Oster

EVERY DAY A GOURMET

The easy-does-it Kitchen Center®way.

by Cynthia and Jerome Rubin

SUNDAY

MONDAY

TUESDAY

WEDNESDAY

THURSDAY

FRIDAY

SATURDAY

Dorison House Publishers, Inc. Boston

ABOUT THE AUTHORS

Cynthia and Jerome Rubin reside in Boston, Massachusetts, a place from which they spend much time testing and sampling good cooking. Cynthia learned about gourmet cooking while living in Paris and attending cooking school, and she and Jerome have been practicing the art ever since. They are the joint authors of the *Proper Bostonian Cookbook, Old Boston Fare, The New Fruit Cookbook* and a series of international cookbooks. They love gourmet cooking and have compiled this collection from among their favorite recipes.

ACKNOWLEDGMENTS

Many thanks to Mary Beth Jung, Director of Home Economics and the Oster Test Kitchen. She and her assistants tested, tasted and gave invaluable advice to insure that each of these recipes makes best use of the Kitchen Center food preparation appliance.

Fifth Printing, 1980

Copyright © 1978 by Dorison House Publishers, Inc.
Published by Dorison House Publishers, Inc.
824 Park Square Bldg., Boston, MA 02116
ISBN: 0-916752-29-1
Library of Congress Number: 78-68223
Manufactured in the United States of America

Book design: Cachalot Design Group   Marblehead, Massachusetts
Illustration: Brian Cody

® Oster Kitchen Center Mini-Blend TM FOODCRAFTER

CONTENTS

INTRODUCTION   5

THE WAY TO SUCCESSFUL FOOD PROCESSING   7

Chapter One   APPETIZERS   11

Chapter Two   BREADS   23

Chapter Three   SOUPS   35

Chapter Four   SALADS AND DRESSINGS   43

Chapter Five   VEGETABLES   57

Chapter Six   MAIN DISHES   67

Chapter Seven   DESSERTS   81

Chapter Eight   BAKED GOODS   91

Chapter Nine   JAMS, JELLIES, PRESERVES   119

Chapter Ten   MISCELLANEOUS   127

            Beverages   128

            Frostings   132

            Sauces   133

            Candies   136

            Crepes   139

            Sausages   140

INDEX   141

INTRODUCTION

Cooking, without a doubt, has become the national pastime. For people of all ages and backgrounds it is both a necessity and a pleasure. Gourmet clubs, cooking classes and innovative kitchen tools and appliances have helped to give impetus to this kitchen renaissance. Both experienced cooks and amateurs are attempting to perfect new taste sensations, sample international cuisines and learn more about the history of gastronomy. In this heightened spirit of culinary adventure and discovery, cooks are daily inspired to try new recipes and techniques.

A creative chef wants to increase the pleasure of preparing interesting new foods. Naturally, the busy cook, no matter how organized, is always looking for a shorter and more efficient way to work. But of all the timesaving kitchen devices, the food processor is easily the most exciting new appliance available today. The many tasks, which are an integral part of cooking, you are now able to accomplish with just one machine.

The Kitchen Center food preparation appliance is the ultimate in food processing on today's market. Imagine! In one compact and space-saving appliance you can blend, mix, grind, slice, cut, shred and make dough. One device takes the place of five and saves you time and money besides. It will also perform numerous functions that many food processors cannot do; namely, beat egg whites, whip cream, make sausage, etc.

Incidentally, you should take advantage of the varied accessories that are available. They will increase your versatility and relieve you of many tedious everyday kitchen chores.

Creative food preparation is now available to everyone. Here is a machine that will do just about everything except eat the food. Even professional chefs who have long advocated chopping and doing other time-consuming tasks by hand, are now enthusiastic about the versatility of this dazzling appliance.

For parties, it saves hours of time. There is less waste; thus, it saves you money. And the everyday cook who could never find the time to make that "special dish" will now discover that every day she can conjure up a gourmet dish. And, indeed, many gourmet specialties are included in this book. How delightful to sample your own homemade breads for breakfast or a hearty cassoulet for dinner! It makes you dream of France in the very boundaries of your own kitchen. Even many dishes that had seemed beyond your horizon are now easy to prepare with so much of the food preparation made so simple.

In order to take best advantage of your food preparation appliance, you should first make sure that you have read and that you understand the instructions for the proper use and maintenance of the unit. This is important because the more you understand its operation, the more you will be able to accomplish with it. This book, however, is not a substitute for the instructions manual you received with the appliance. It will give you years of trouble-free service if you operate it according to the instructions.

It will also be easier to get accustomed to your new food processor if you make sure from the very beginning that it is kept on the kitchen counter within easy reach. Make a special effort to use it as much as possible. In that way, you'll not only get more practice, but you'll break the old habits of hand chopping, slicing, grinding, etc.

And just think! Now you'll be saving money because you can bypass many processed supermarket and "take-out" foods that you may have relied upon for last-minute guests, a lazy evening in, or an easy way to throw a festive party. You can dine on the highest quality gourmet food at home with a minimum of expense. And in times of rising inflation, that is a useful and necessary consideration.

But most important is that now you will experience excellent results in an area which is an extension of your own personality. Accordingly, we have selected recipes to give a maximum of eating pleasure with a minimum of work. So read on! You're on your way to becoming a gourmet every day.

THE WAY
TO SUCCESSFUL
FOOD PROCESSING

First, read carefully the instruction booklet that comes with your appliance. Here are some reminders:

- Turn the Blender off before using the rubber scraper to push down ingredients.
- Empty heavy mixtures through the base of the jar to remove all the ingredients.
- Grate cheese in the Blender refrigerator-cold.
- To grate lemon or orange peel in the Blender, freeze thin strips of peel, then process ½ cup at a time in the Mini-Blend container at BLEND.
- Fresh coconut can be grated in the Blender with the speed set at LIQUEFY. Remove the feeder cap, start the motor and drop pieces of coconut into the revolving blades. Grate 1½ cups of coconut at a time.
- To grind poppy seed for filling, place ½ cup of poppy seeds in "Mini-Blend" container and process at GRIND until seeds are crushed and moist. Stop the Blender once or twice to shake the seeds down from the top of the container.
- When slicing narrow foods like celery, carrots or cucumbers, pack the food hopper firmly, and press food onto Slicer Disc with the Food Pusher.
- Cut long narrow vegetables to about the length of the Food Pusher to get even slices.
- To shred Mozzarella or Swiss cheeses using the Shredder Disc be sure they are ice cold.
- Choose firm, fresh fruits and vegetables for processing.

Due to variations in size, consistency, age and temperature of foods to be processed, it may be necessary to increase or decrease speeds referred to in the recipes. Owners of 12-speed units may find it necessary to adjust recipes by increasing speeds by 1 or 2. The recipes in this book call for some special procedures using the Blender. The following charts can be your guide to those processes:

BLENDER-CHOP (WATER METHOD)

(Chopping 2-4 cups fruits and vegetables)

Cut vegetables into pieces about 1 inch in size and place recommended quantity in blender container. Cover vegetables with cold water, cover container and process for number of cycles indicated:

Food	Quantity	Speed	Cycles	Finished Quantity
Apples	3 cups	MIX	2	2 cups grated
Cabbage, red	3 cups	GRIND	1	1-1/2 cups
Cabbage, white	3 cups	GRIND	1	1-1/2 cups
Carrots	2 cups	LIQUEFY	1	2 cups
Green Pepper	3 cups	CHOP	1	1-1/2 cups
Onion	3 cups	GRIND	1	1-1/3 cups
Potatoes	3 cups	GRIND	1	2 cups

When processing is finished, immediately pour through a strainer or colander and drain well.

The speeds and number of cycles listed above produce a medium-size chop. If a finer size is desired, process one additional cycle.

BLENDER-CHOP (DRY METHOD)

(Chopping 1 cup or less)

Cut foods into pieces about 1-inch in size and place recommended quantity in blender container or in Mini-Blend container (1/2 cup only). Process for number of cycles indicated: DO NOT use Mini-Blend container to process cheese.

Food	Quantity	Speed	Cycles	Finished Quantity
Apples	1 cup	STIR	2	3/4 cup
Carrots	1 cup	CHOP	2	1 cup
Celery	1 cup	CHOP	2-3	3/4 cup
Green Pepper	1 cup	STIR	2	2/3 cup
Onion	1 cup	PUREE	2	3/4 cup
Cheese, Cheddar	1/2 cup	GRIND	3	1/2 cup
Cheese, Swiss	1 cup	GRIND	4	1 cup
Eggs, hard-cooked	2	STIR	2	3/4 cup

Nuts—1/2 cup in Mini-Blend or 1 cup in large container

Food	Quantity	Speed	Cycles	Finished Quantity
Peanuts		WHIP	3	
Almonds		MIX	4	
Pecans		WHIP	2	
Walnuts		WHIP	2	

BLENDER-CRUMB

Bread—Tear one slice of fresh, plain or buttered, bread into 8 pieces, put into blender container, cover and process for number of cycles indicated:

Bread

Coarse	1 slice	STIR	1	1/2 cup
Regular	1 slice	GRATE	2	1/2 cup
Fine	1 slice	LIQUEFY	Continuous	1/2 cup

Crackers, Cookies—Break crackers and cookies into blender container, cover and process for number of cycles indicated:

Zwieback	6	GRIND	4	1/2 cup
Graham Crackers	8	GRIND	3	1/2 cup
Soda Crackers	16	GRIND	2	1/2 cup
Chocolate Wafers	10	GRIND	3	1/2 cup
Small Coconut Cookies	8	GRIND	3	1/2 cup
Vanilla Wafers	16	GRATE	3	1/2 cup

If finer size is desired, process one additional cycle.

BLENDER-GRIND

Nuts	Rice	Peppercorns	Coffee Beans
Oats	Wheat	Whole Spices	

Put 1/2 cup in Mini-Blend container or 1 cup in the blender container, cover and process at GRIND until desired grind is obtained. Longer processing will give a finer grind. **NOTE:** Whole ginger root and nutmeg are extremely hard spices, and it is recommended that only two or three 1-inch pieces of ginger or 3 nutmegs be processed at one time. Break nutmeg with a nutcracker before processing. Process only in glass blender container at LIQUEFY. Coffee beans are quickly and evenly ground, 1/2 cup at a time, in Mini-Blend.

GRIND — 10 cycles for percolator
GRIND — 15 cycles for drip

BLENDER-GRATE
Semi-Hard, Hard Cheese (Refrigerator Cold)

Cover and turn Kitchen Center blender to BLEND. With motor on, remove feeder cap and drop no more than 1 cup of 1-inch cheese cubes into container. Push "OFF" button. Remove cheese through bottom of blender container. Repeat if necessary.

RECONSTITUTE

Frozen Concentrated Juices and Soups—Always put water (liquid) into the blender container first. Put frozen concentrate in the liquid. Cover container and hold jar while processing at STIR only until well mixed.

Dry Milk—Put water and dry milk solids into the blender container, cover and process at STIR only until well mixed.

LIQUEFY

Fruits, Vegetables and Other Solid Foods with Addition of a Liquid—The blender is not a juice extractor, but it will break down the fibrous parts of vegetable and fruit pieces so that all the flavor is released into a liquid. This liquid may be water or any prepared fruit or vegetable juice. Use the following table only as a guide—you may want a thicker or thinner juice.

Amount of Fruit or Vegetable	Amount of Liquid	Yield
1 medium apple, peeled, cored, cut in eighths	1 cup	About 1-1/2 cups
3 small carrots, cut in 1-inch pieces	1 cup	About 1-1/2 cups
2 large celery stalks, cut in 1-inch pieces	1 cup	About 1-1/2 cups

Place ingredients in blender container, cover and process at LIQUEFY until pieces of food are no longer visible. Remove feeder cap and add 3 or 4 ice cubes, one at a time, to thoroughly chill liquid. Continue processing until cubes are dissolved. (If desired, this juice may be strained through a fine sieve to remove the small fibrous particles.)

Due to variations in size, consistency and age of food items, it may be necessary to increase or decrease the number of cycles indicated in this chart and in the recipes throughout the book to achieve desired results.

Chapter One
APPETIZERS

SHRIMP PASTE

2 tablespoons (30 ml) chili sauce
2 tablespoons (30 ml) mayonnaise
1 tablespoon (15 ml) lemon juice

Dash curry powder
1 can (5 ounces or 140 g) shrimp, drained
Watercress sprigs

Assemble Blender. Put all ingredients into blender container. Cover and process at LIQUEFY until smooth. If necessary, STOP BLENDER, using rubber spatula to keep mixture around the processing blades. Spread on bread canapes or crackers. Garnish with sprigs of watercress.
Yield: 3/4 cup (200 ml)

CHEESE BALL

1 cup green olive pieces, drained
1 package (12 ounces or 336 g) Cheddar cheese, cubed
1 package (8 ounces or 227 g) cream cheese, softened

1 container (8 ounces or 227 g) smoke-flavored Cheddar or processed cheese spread
1 teaspoon (5 ml) Worcestershire sauce
1/2 teaspoon (2 ml) dry mustard
Chopped parsley or nuts

Assemble Grinder with Fine Disc. Grind olives and Cheddar cheese cubes into large mixer bowl. Assemble Mixer. Add remaining ingredients to olives and cheese and mix at #4 until creamy and well mixed. Cover bowl and chill thoroughly. Shape chilled mixture into ball. Roll in parsley or nuts. Serve with assorted crackers or bread sticks.
Yield: 1 cheese ball, 1-1/2 pounds (680 g)

CHEESE SOUFFLE

1/2 pound (227 g) Cheddar cheese, cubed
3 tablespoons (45 ml) butter
3 tablespoons (45 ml) flour

1 cup (250 ml) milk
Dash cayenne pepper
6 eggs, separated

Assemble Blender. Blender-grate Cheddar cheese. Set aside. Melt butter in top of double boiler. Stir in flour. Cook one minute. Add milk, stirring constantly until mixture is thick. Stir grated Cheddar cheese into mixture, and continue stirring until sauce becomes smooth. Add cayenne pepper, and stir again. Set aside top of double boiler until it is cool. Assemble Mixer. In small mixer bowl beat egg yolks at #7 until thick and creamy. Add to the cheese sauce, and beat until well blended. Cook about 15 minutes.

Preheat oven to 350° F. (180° C.). Beat egg whites in large mixer bowl at #9 until they stand in peaks, but are not hard or dry. Stir about a quarter of the egg whites into the cheese sauce. Mixture will be slightly foamy. Then fold remaining egg whites into cheese mixture, distributing them evenly without breaking them down. Pour mixture into buttered 10-inch (25 cm) souffle dish. Bake about 25 minutes. Souffle will rise high and be golden brown on top.
Yield: 4 servings

HERRING PATE

1 jar (12 ounces or 336 g) herring
    in wine sauce, drained
1 package (8 ounces or 227 g) cream
    cheese

1/2 cup (125 ml) pitted ripe olives
1/3 cup (75 ml) chopped parsley
1/2 teaspoon (2 ml) curry powder
Juice of half a lemon

Assemble Blender. Put all ingredients into blender container. Cover and process at BLEND until smooth. Place mixture into a crock or earthenware deep dish. Cover and chill until ready to serve. Serve with dark bread rounds, bread sticks or crackers.
Yield: 3 cups (750 ml)

MARINATED MUSHROOMS

1 pound (454 g) fresh mushrooms
3/4 cup (200 ml) salad oil
1 medium onion
2 cloves garlic
1 teaspoon (5 ml) sugar

3/4 cup (150 ml) red wine vinegar
1/2 cup (125 ml) parsley flakes
Boston lettuce leaves
Watercress sprigs

Assemble Salad Maker with Thin Slicer. Slice mushrooms and place in a glass bowl. Assemble Blender. Put remaining ingredients into blender container. Cover and process at WHIP. Pour over sliced mushrooms. Cover and marinate several hours in refrigerator, stirring occasionally. To serve, arrange lettuce leaves and watercress on a large platter or individual salad bowls. Remove mushrooms from marinade with a slotted spoon; mound in center of platter or bowl, and pour marinate over.
Yield: 10-12 servings

ANTIPASTO PLATTER

1/4 pound (113 g) sliced salami
1/4 pound (113 g) sliced cooked ham
1/4 pound (113 g) mushrooms, sliced
    or 1 (4-ounce or 113 g) can whole
    mushrooms, drained

1 (5-ounce or 140 g) can ripe olives
Cherry tomatoes, about 10
Scallions, about 5
2 apples, cored and cut into wedges
Snappy Cheese Dip

Arrange sliced meats, vegetables and apples on round platter. Serve with Snappy Cheese Dip.

Snappy Cheese Dip

1/2 cup (125 ml) milk
1 (8-ounce or 227 g) package cream
    cheese, at room temperature
1/4 pound (113 g) Cheddar cheese, cubed

1/4 cup plus 2 tablespoons (80 ml) milk
1 clove garlic, crushed
1/4 teaspoon (1 ml) salt

Assemble Blender. Place all ingredients in blender container. Cover and process at BLEND until smooth. Serve at room temperature.
Yield: 4 servings

CHICKEN LIVER PATE

3 cups (750 ml) water
6 sprigs parsley
1 stalk celery with leaves
8 peppercorns
1/4 teaspoon (1 ml) tarragon
1/2 pound (227 g) chicken livers
1/2 teaspoon (2 ml) salt
Dash cayenne pepper

1 teaspoon (5 ml) dry mustard
1/2 teaspoon (2 ml) nutmeg
1 clove garlic, crushed
3 tablespoons (45 ml) chopped onion
1/4 pound (113 g) butter, softened
2 hard-cooked eggs, coarsely chopped
2 tablespoons (30 ml) melted butter

In a saucepan bring water to boiling; add parsley, celery, peppercorns and tarragon. Simmer 5 minutes. Add chicken livers; cover and cook 10 minutes. Remove livers, and cut into small pieces. Assemble Blender. Put livers, a few at a time, into blender container, and process at PUREE until smooth. Add all remaining ingredients except melted butter and process at MIX only until eggs are finely chopped. Pour into a terrine and cover with melted butter; chill. Mixture will be thin but will become firm when chilled. Serve with assorted crackers or Melba toast.
Yield: 6-8 servings

SMOKY EGG SPREAD

4 green onions
1 tablespoon (15 ml) butter
6 hard-cooked eggs
1/3 cup (75 ml) mayonnaise

2 teaspoons (10 ml) prepared mustard
1/4 teaspoon (1 ml) dried dill
3 dashes hot pepper sauce
1/2 teaspoon (2 ml) hickory smoked salt

Trim onions. Cut off all but 2 inches (5 cm) from the green ends. Assemble Blender. Blender chop. Set aside. Saute onion in butter until soft but not browned. Put with eggs, mayonnaise, mustard, dill, hot pepper sauce and hickory smoked salt into blender container. Cover and process at BLEND until smooth. Turn out into serving bowl. Chill before serving. This is excellent on cocktail rye bread or toast points.
Yield: 1-3/4 cups (450 ml)

TOMATO PROVENCALE

8 tomatoes
1 slice white bread
1 clove garlic
4 tablespoons (60 ml) fresh basil or parsley

1/4 teaspoon (1 ml) salt
Dash pepper
4 tablespoons (60 ml) butter

The day before: Cut off a thick slice of tomato from the stem ends. Turn upside down, and gently squeeze out tomato juice and seed. Assemble Blender. Blender-crumb bread with garlic and basil or parsley. Add seasoning, and fill each tomato cup with some of this mixture. Dot each with butter, and place in a greased, oven-proof pan. Refrigerate until 15 minutes before serving. Bake in 400° F. (200° C.) oven for about 15 minutes, or until hot and browned on top.
Yield: 8 servings

LIPTAUER CHEESE

This Hungarian recipe has become a favorite for the American cocktail hour. Its taste is not easy to describe but it's definitely worth trying! Its popularity will vouch for that.

1/2 pound (227 g) cottage cheese
1/2 pound (227 g) butter
1/2 teaspoon (2 ml) anchovy paste
2 tablespoons (30 ml) chopped capers
1-1/2 tablespoons (22 ml) caraway
    seeds

2 tablespoons (30 ml) minced chives
1-1/2 tablespoons (22 ml) prepared
    mustard
1-1/2 tablespoons (22 ml) paprika
Salt to taste
1 clove garlic, halved

Assemble Mixer. Cream the cottage cheese and butter together at #4 until smooth and well blended. Work in all the other ingredients except the salt and garlic. Add a little salt after mixing, if needed. Rub a 4-cup (1000 ml) crock or serving bowl with the cut clove of garlic and firmly pack cheese into it. Chill overnight, or about 5 hours before serving. Serve with cocktail rye bread or Westphalian pumpernickel.
Yield: 10-12 servings

EGGPLANT SALAD SPREAD

An Old World tradition.

2 pounds (1 kg) eggplant
2 tablespoons (30 ml) red wine vinegar
2 tablespoons (30 ml) olive oil
1 teaspoon (5 ml) sweet basil
1/2 teaspoon (2 ml) oregano

1 teaspoon (5 ml) salt
Dash pepper
2 garlic cloves
3 sprigs parsley
1 tomato, cut in 1-inch (2.5 cm) chunks

In a 350° F. (180° C.) oven bake eggplants whole until soft, about 40 minutes or bake in a microwave oven 6-10 minutes. Peel and cube. Put the vinegar, oil, seasonings, parsley and half the tomato and eggplant into the blender container, cover and process at BLEND until smooth. Add remaining tomato and eggplant. Cover and pulse at GRIND until finely chopped. Serve chilled with crusty French or Italian bread as an appetizer spread.
Yield: 4 cups (1 liter)

POTTED SHRIMP

Potted foods are from the English tradition. The word is often used to describe meat, poultry or fish ground into a fine paste, seasoned and packed. Many types of cheese are potted, often with wines or brandy. They are then served in a small pot or earthenware dish.

1 pound (454 g) shrimp, cooked,
    shelled and deveined
1 small onion
1/2 cup (125 ml) butter, softened

Worcestershire sauce
Celery salt
Cayenne pepper

Assemble Food Grinder with Fine Disc. Grind shrimp. Peel onion and grind. Mix ground shrimp and onion with butter and season to taste with Worcestershire sauce, celery salt and cayenne pepper. Chill until firm.
Yield: 8-10 servings

STUFFED MUSHROOMS

12 to 16 large fresh mushrooms
1 small green pepper
1 small onion
1-1/2 cups (375 ml) fresh breadcrumbs

1/8 teaspoon (1/2 ml) pepper
1/2 cup (125 ml) butter
1/2 teaspoon (1 ml) salt
Dash of cayenne

Preheat oven to 350° F. (180° C.). Wipe mushrooms with a damp cloth. Remove stems. Assemble Blender. Put mushroom stems, cut up green pepper and onion in blender container. Blender-chop finely. Heat 3 tablespoons (45 ml) butter in a large skillet. Saute mushroom caps, bottoms only, 2 to 3 minutes. Remove and arrange, rounded side down, in a shallow baking dish. Heat the rest of the butter in the same skillet. Saute chopped stems, green pepper and onion until tender (about 5 minutes). Remove from heat. Stir in bread crumbs and seasonings. Use to fill mushroom caps, mounding high in the center. Bake 15 minutes.
Yield: 6-8 servings

SEVICHE

Many versions of this seafood cocktail appear throughout Mexico and Latin America. In Acapulco, this is a specialty made with red snapper. It is an unusual way to begin a "gourmet" happening.

2 pounds (1 kg) halibut or other white
    fish fillets, fresh or frozen
2 teaspoons (10 ml) grated lemon peel
1-1/2 cups (375 ml) lemon juice
1 cup (250 ml) finely chopped onion

2 medium tomatoes, peeled, seeded
    and drained
Salt
Few drops hot sauce, optional

Thaw fish, if frozen. With sharp knife, slice fillets at a 45° angle into paper-thin slices that partially fall apart. The fish should appear almost grated. Drain well to yield 4 cups. Place in shallow glass bowl; stir in lemon peel. Add lemon juice gradually, stirring with a fork and working until juice is almost completely absorbed. Let stand 20 minutes until mixture turns white. Stir occasionally. Assemble Blender. Blender-chop onions and then tomatoes, enough to make 1/2 cup (125 ml). Stir into fish mixture. Season to taste with salt and hot sauce, if desired. Cover and refrigerate until well chilled. Before serving, drain off any excess liquid. Serve with corn chips.
Yield: 10-12 servings

SHRIMP MARINADE

4 tablespoons (60 ml) vinegar
4 tablespoons (60 ml) salad oil
4 tablespoons (60 ml) chili sauce

1/4 teaspoon (1 ml) garlic salt
1 teaspoon (5 ml) prepared mustard
1 pound (454 g) jumbo shrimp, cooked

    Assemble Blender. Put all ingredients except shrimp into the blender container. Cover and process at MIX until smooth. Pour over shrimp and toss to coat with sauce. Marinate overnight.
Yield: 3/4 cup (200 ml)

WALNUT CLAM ROLL

1-1/4 cups (300 ml) chopped toasted* walnuts
1 can (8 ounces or 227 g) minced clams, well drained
2 packages (8 ounces or 227 g each) cream cheese, softened

2 tablespoons (30 ml) finely chopped onion
2 tablespoons (30 ml) lemon juice
Garlic salt to taste

    Assemble Blender. Blender-chop (dry method) the walnuts. Drain clams well. Assemble Mixer. In large mixer bowl beat cheese and clams together at #4 until smooth. Beat in onion, lemon juice and garlic salt to taste. Stir in 1/2 cup of the walnuts. Turn mixture out onto wax paper. Shape into one or two logs, about 2-inches (5 cm) in diameter, by rolling back and forth. Roll in remaining walnuts until surface is well coated. Cover with foil and chill several hours until firm. Cut into slices to serve.
Yield: 3 dozen

To toast walnuts, spread nuts evenly in shallow pan. Bake at 350° F. (180° C.), stirring often, for 12-15 minutes, or until golden brown. Cool.

LOW-CAL COTTAGE CHEESE DIP BASE

5 tablespoons (75 ml) milk
1 tablespoon (15 ml) lemon juice

1 cup (250 ml) creamed cottage cheese

Assemble Blender. Put ingredients into blender container, cover and process at BLEND until smooth and creamy. Use as a base for dips or in place of sour cream. Serve with assorted crisp vegetable strips.
Yield: 1 cup (250 ml)

GUACAMOLE DIP

3 tablespoons (45 ml) lemon juice
1 medium tomato, quartered
1 small onion, quartered
2-4 small jalapeno peppers

1 teaspoon (5 ml) monosodium glutamate
1 teaspoon (5 ml) salt
2 large ripe avocados, cut in pieces

Assemble Blender. Put all ingredients into blender container, cover and process at BLEND until smooth. If necessary, STOP BLENDER, use rubber spatula to keep mixture around the processing blades. Serve with corn chips, crackers or raw vegetables.
Yield: 2 cups (500 ml)

HOT SAUSAGES

Serve any sausages hot in a chafing dish or electrically heated tray. Kielbasa sausages or Rose's Country Sausage (see page 140) are ideal to serve in this way....
Heat 1-inch long sausages in red or white wine which has been flavored with chopped onion. Serve with mustard or barbecue sauce.

CASHEW BUTTER

2 tablespoons (30 ml) vegetable oil   1-1/2 cups (375 ml) cashews

Assemble Blender. Put vegetable oil into blender container. Add nuts, cover and process at BLEND until a crunchy or smooth consistency is reached. If necessary STOP BLENDER, use rubber spatula to keep mixture around the processing blades. If unsalted nuts are used, add salt for flavor. Use as hors d'oeuvre spread on crackers or cocktail bread.
Yield: 1 cup (250 ml)

STEAK TARTARE

Popular in Holland and France, steak tartare is served more and more in this country. It may be served with a choice of favorite chopped vegetables, such as onions, green peppers, radishes and capers.

2 pounds (1 kg) tenderloin steak   Pepper to taste
10 anchovy fillets   Dash hot pepper sauce
1 medium onion, quartered   1 tablespoon (15 ml) Dijon mustard
2 egg yolks   2 tablespoons (30 ml) cognac, optional
1 teaspoon (5 ml) salt

Assemble Food Grinder with Fine Disc. Grind tenderloin steak. Assemble Blender. Put remaining ingredients into blender container and blender-chop. Pour over the ground meat and combine thoroughly. Keep chilled and covered until ready to serve. Serve in a mound with crackers or slices of bread.
Yield: 8-10 servings

SPINACH WATER CHESTNUT CANAPE

1 10-ounce (283 g) package frozen
chopped spinach
1/2 can (4 ounces or 113 g) water
chestnuts
2 tablespoons (30 ml) mayonnaise

1 tablespoon (15 ml) sour cream
3 scallions or 1 small onion
1/4 teaspoon (1 ml) salt
Freshly ground pepper

Thaw spinach and press free of water. Assemble Blender. Place spinach, water chestnuts, mayonnaise, sour cream and onion in blender container. Process at PUREE, increasing speed until mixture is almost smooth. STOP BLENDER and use rubber spatula to push ingredients down into blades often. Chill. Serve on very crisp crackers.
Yield: About 1-1/4 cups (300 ml)

CANAPES AU FROMAGE

These crisp cheese wafers make an excellent cocktail snack. Once you start eating them it is very hard to stop. The onion salt and celery seeds give them a piquant flavor.

Sharp Cheddar cheese, cubed
2 cups (500 ml) all-purpose flour
2 teaspoons (10 ml) onion salt

1/2 teaspoon (2 ml) celery seed
3/4 cup (200 ml) shortening
2 tablespoons (30 ml) water

Assemble Blender. Blender-grate Cheddar cheese to make 1 cup. In large mixer bowl combine grated cheese with flour, onion salt and celery seed. Cut in shortening until mixture is coarse. Assemble Doughmaker. Gradually work in water to form a soft dough. Divide dough in half; roll between wax paper to 1/4-inch (0.6 cm) thickness. Cut into circles 3-inches (8 cm) in diameter. Place on ungreased cookie sheet. Prick well with fork. Bake at 425° F. (220° C.) about 8-10 minutes until golden. Turn onto wire racks to cool.
Yield: 3 dozen

Chapter Two
BREADS

CANADIAN OATCAKES

6 cups (1500 ml) rolled oats
3 cups (750 ml) all-purpose flour
1 cup (250 ml) sugar
1 teaspoon (5 ml) salt

1/2 teaspoon (2 ml) baking soda
2 cups (500 ml) shortening
5 tablespoons (75 ml) cold water
Whole wheat flour

Preheat oven to 375° F. (190° C.). Assemble Mixer. In large mixer bowl mix at #1 oats, flour, sugar, salt and baking soda together until evenly blended. Add shortening until mixture resembles coarse meal. Add water, one tablespoon (15 ml) at a time, and mix as little as possible. Form into ball. Flour a board with whole wheat flour and form dough into two balls. Roll each into a rectangle about 1/4-inch (0.6 cm) thick. Cut into 3-inch (8 cm) squares. Bake 15-20 mintues, or until slightly browned on top. These may be baked a day before serving for good results.
Yield: 4-5 dozen

BUTTERSCOTCH BREAD

This innovative bread is rich and delicious. The topping adds an extra-special crunchy texture.

1 cup (250 ml) walnuts
2 tablespoons (30 ml) sesame seed
2 tablespoons (30 ml) sugar
1/4 teaspoon (1 ml) cinnamon
1/4 teaspoon (1 ml) nutmeg
2 cups (500 ml) sifted all-purpose
    flour
1 teaspoon (5 ml) baking powder

1/2 teaspoon (2 ml) baking soda
1 teaspoon (5 ml) salt
2 eggs
1 cup (250 ml) firmly packed dark
    brown sugar
3 tablespoons (45 ml) butter, melted
1 cup (250 ml) buttermilk

Assemble Blender. Blender-chop walnuts. Set aside. In a measuring cup, combine sesame seed, sugar, cinnamon and nutmeg. Set aside for topping. Sift the flour in the small mixing bowl with baking powder, soda and salt. Set aside. Assemble Mixer. In large mixer bowl beat the eggs at #4 slightly. Add the brown sugar and melted butter. Mix well. Add the flour mixture alternately with the buttermilk, stirring just until blended. Add chopped nuts. Pour into well-greased 5 x 9-inch (13 x 23 cm) loaf pan. Sprinkle the top with the sesame seed mixture. Bake at 350° F. (180° C.) for about 1 hour, or until the bread starts to move away from sides of pan. Serve warm or cooled.
Yield: 1 loaf

SWEET CORN BREAD

Delicious when hot, this sweet and flavorful bread is also tasty and tender after cooling.

3/4 cup (200 ml) sugar
1/2 cup (125 ml) salad oil
2 eggs, beaten
1-1/2 cups (375 ml) sifted all-purpose flour

3 teaspoons (15 ml) baking powder
Dash salt
1-1/2 cups (375 ml) yellow cornmeal
1 cup (250 ml) milk

Assemble Mixer. In large mixer bowl blend sugar and salad oil. Beat in eggs at #4. Sift flour again with baking powder and salt; add cornmeal. Combine the dry ingredients with the creamed mixture alternately with the milk. Pour into a greased, floured 9-inch (23 cm) square pan. Bake at 400° F. (200° C.) for 30 minutes.
Yield: 6 servings

ORANGE PRUNE NUT LOAF

A quick bread that is delicate and orange flavored. And, you'll find plump bits of prunes and nuts for added texture.

1-1/4 cup (300 ml) pecans
1 medium orange, quartered and seeded
1/2 cup (125 ml) orange juice
1 teaspoon (5 ml) baking soda
1 cup (250 ml) cooked pitted prunes, drained
2/3 cup (175 ml) sugar

1 egg
1 tablespoon (15 ml) melted butter
1/2 teaspoon (2 ml) vanilla extract
2 cups (500 ml) sifted all-purpose flour
2-1/2 teaspoons (12 ml) baking powder
1/2 teaspoon (2 ml) salt

Assemble Blender. Blender-chop nuts. Put into a bowl. Cut orange into chunks. Put into blender container along with the orange juice. Cover and blend until pureed. Empty into a saucepan; add the baking soda. Bring to a boil. Return mixture to blender container, add prunes and blender-chop. Assemble Mixer.

In a large mixer bowl combine sugar, egg, melted butter and vanilla extract. Beat at #4 until smooth. Sift together flour, baking powder and salt. Add to creamed mixture all at once along with the orange puree mixture. Stir until batter is well blended. Add nuts to batter. Pour into greased 9 x 5 x 3-inch (23 x 13 x 8 cm) loaf pan. Bake at 300° F. (150° C.) for 1 hour and 10 minutes, or until loaf tests done. Let stand 5 minutes before turning onto wire rack to cool. Tightly wrap with foil and store overnight in refrigerator to keep fresh.
Yield: 1 loaf

FRENCH DOUGHNUTS

French doughnuts or beignets are traditionally made in France, like the American fritter, with foods such as fish, chicken or vegetables. In New Orleans, they are the trademark of the coffeehouses of the French Market and often are served with New Orleans' famous coffee with chicory.

2-3/4 to 3-1/4 cups (700-800 ml)
    all-purpose flour
1 package (1/4 ounce or 7 g) active
    dry yeast
1 teaspoon (5 ml) ground nutmeg
1 cup (250 ml) milk

1/4 cup (50 ml) sugar
1/4 cup (50 ml) vegetable oil
1/2 teaspoon (2 ml) salt
1 egg
Oil for frying
Sifted confectioners' sugar

Assemble Mixer. In a large mixer bowl combine 1-1/2 cups (375 ml) flour, yeast and nutmeg. Heat milk, sugar, oil and salt just until warm (about 120° F. or 48° C.). Add to dry ingredients along with the egg and mix at #2 about a minute, scraping bowl constantly. Then beat at #6 for about 3 minutes. Remove beaters and replace with dough hooks. Add remaining flour at #10 until thoroughly mixed. It will be a sticky dough. Place in greased bowl; turn once. Cover and chill. Turn dough out onto floured surface. Cover; let rest 10 minutes. Roll to 18 x 12-inch (45 x 31 cm) rectangle. Cut into 3 x 2-inch (8 x 5 cm) rectangles. Cover; let rise 30 minutes. Dough will not double. Fry in deep hot oil or fat at 375° F. (190° C.) until golden, turning once. Drain. Sprinkle with confectioners' sugar. Best served warm.
Yield: 3 dozen

SOUR CREAM CRESCENTS

1 cup (250 ml) sour cream
2 tablespoons (30 ml) sugar
1 teaspoon (5 ml) salt
1/4 cup (50 ml) melted shortening
1 package (1/4 ounce or 7 g) active
    dry yeast

1/4 cup (50 ml) lukewarm water
1 egg, beaten
3-3/4 cups (950 ml) sifted all-purpose
    flour, approximately
Butter, melted

Warm sour cream in top of a double boiler. When lukewarm, remove from heat and add sugar, salt and melted shortening. Assemble Doughmaker. Soften yeast in the lukewarm water and put in large mixer bowl with sour cream mixture. Add beaten egg. Beat in two cups of flour. Stir in the remaining flour to make a rather soft dough, yet stiff enough to handle. Cover and let rise in a warm place until doubled. This takes 1 hour and 45 minutes.

Turn out on a floured board and knead lightly until smooth. Divide dough in half. Use a rolling pin to shape each half into a circle about 1/2-inch (1 cm) thick and cut in about twelve wedge-shaped pieces. Brush each wedge with melted butter and roll it, beginning from wide side, pulling each point and tucking it under so crescent will not unroll in oven. Place on a greased cookie sheet. Cover and let rise until doubled. (Approximately an hour.) Bake at 375° F. (190° C.) for 20 minutes.
Yield: 2 dozen

MOLASSES CORN BREAD

1 cup (250 ml) whole bran
1 cup (250 ml) milk
1/2 cup (125 ml) shortening
1/2 cup (125 ml) sugar
2 eggs

1/2 cup (125 ml) molasses
1 cup (250 ml) all-purpose flour
3 teaspoons (15 ml) baking powder
1/2 teaspoon (2 ml) salt
1/2 cup (125 ml) yellow cornmeal

Assemble Mixer. In small mixer bowl combine whole bran and milk. Set aside. In large mixer bowl cream shortening and sugar at #4 until light and fluffy. Beat in eggs, just until blended. Stir in molasses and bran mixture. Stir together flour, baking powder and salt; add cornmeal. Add dry ingredients to creamed mixture, stirring just until blended. Pour into greased 9 x 9 x 2-inch (23 x 23 x 5 cm) baking pan. Bake at 375° F. (190° C.) about 30 minutes or until done. Cut into squares to serve.
Yield: 6-8 servings

MAPLE DOUGHNUT HOLES

2 cups (500 ml) sifted all-purpose flour
3-1/2 teaspoons (17 ml) baking powder
1 teaspoon (5 ml) salt
1/2 teaspoon (2 ml) nutmeg
1/4 cup (50 ml) shortening
1/4 cup (50 ml) sugar
1 egg
3/4 cup (200 ml) milk
Oil for frying, about 2 inches (5 cm) deep
Maple Glaze

Heat oil to 375° F. (190° C.). Prepare Maple Glaze and set aside. On a sheet of waxed paper resift the flour with baking powder, salt and nutmeg. Set aside. Assemble Mixer. Combine shortening, sugar and egg in a large mixing bowl and beat at #4 until smooth. Remove the beaters from the mixer arm and replace with dough hooks. Add flour mixture and milk and mix at #10 to a moderately stiff dough. Drop dough by rounded teaspoonfulls into hot oil, and fry until golden brown, about 3 minutes, turning frequently. Remove with a slotted spoon and drain well on paper towels. When all are cooked, dip, one at a time, into Maple Glaze. Allow excess to drip off; then place on a wire rack set over a cookie sheet until glaze is set.

Maple Glaze

1 pound (454 g) confectioners' sugar
6 tablespoons (90 ml) boiling water
1/2 teaspoon (2 ml) maple flavoring

Assemble Mixer. In small mixer bowl, mix at #4 confectioners' sugar with boiling water and maple flavoring. Blend well.
Yield: 3-1/2 dozen

SALLY LUNN

There are many stories told of the origin of Sally Lunn. One is that it is a kind of bun named after an English girl in Bath. Another story says the words "sun" and "moon" in French "soleil" and "lune" were used to describe the brown tops and white bottoms of the rolls. Today it is served baked either in a Turk's head mold or in a square cake pan.

1 package (1/4 ounce or 7 g) active
   dry yeast
1/2 cup (125 ml) very warm water
1 cup (250 ml) milk, scalded
1/4 cup (50 ml) sugar

2 teaspoons (10 ml) salt
1/2 cup (125 ml) butter, softened
3 eggs, beaten
4-1/2 cups (1125 ml) all-purpose flour
Sugar

Preheat oven to 400° F. (200° C.). Sprinkle dry yeast into very warm water (about 110° F. or 40° C.). Let stand for a few minutes. Then stir until dissolved. In large mixer bowl pour milk over sugar, salt and butter. Cool to lukewarm. Add yeast, eggs and flour. Assemble Mixer and beat at #4 until smooth. Cover and let rise until doubled, about 1 hour. Stir down. Pour into two well-greased 8-inch (20 cm) square cake pans. Cover and let rise until doubled, about 30 minutes. Sprinkle each loaf with some sugar. Bake for 25 minutes.
Yield: 2 cakes

WALNUT TEA BREAD

Eat one now and keep the other in the freezer.

6 cups (1500 ml) sifted all-purpose
   flour
2 cups (500 ml) sugar
8 teaspoons (40 ml) baking powder
3 teaspoons (15 ml) salt
2 eggs

1/2 cup (125 ml) melted butter or
   margarine
3 cups (750 ml) milk
2 teaspoons (10 ml) vanilla
3 cups (750 ml) walnuts

Sift dry ingredients into large mixer bowl. Quickly add all remaining liquid ingredients. Assemble Doughmaker. Mix only until dry ingredients are moistened. Add walnuts, mix evenly. Bake in 2 greased 9 x 5 x 3-inch (23 x 13 x 7 cm) pans in preheated 350° F. oven until done, about 1 hour and 20 minutes. Remove from pans and cool on wire rack.
Yield: 2 loaves

HERB BATTER BREAD

1 cup (250 ml) milk, scalded
2 tablespoons (30 ml) sugar
1 tablespoon (15 ml) salt
2 packages (1/4 ounce or 7 g each)
   active dry yeast
1 cup (250 ml) warm water
3 tablespoons (45 ml) chopped parsley

1-1/2 teaspoons (7 ml) crushed sweet basil
1-1/2 teaspoons (7 ml) tarragon leaves
Dash garlic powder
4-1/2 cups (1125 ml) sifted all-purpose
   flour
1 cup (250 ml) walnuts

Mix together milk, sugar and salt. Assemble Mixer. In large mixer bowl sprinkle yeast over water; stir until dissolved. Beat at #4, blending in milk mixture, parsley, basil, tarragon, garlic powder and flour. Continue beating until batter is satiny. Cover and let rise in warm place until double in bulk, about 45 minutes. Assemble Blender. Coarsely chop walnuts. Add walnuts and stir batter down. Beat vigorously with wooden spoon about 1 minute. Pour into lightly greased 1-1/2-quart (1.5 liter) casserole. Bake, uncovered, at 375° F. (190° C.) for 1 hour or until done. Turn out of casserole and cool on rack.
Yield: 1 loaf

SQUASH BREAD

Lightly spiced, this wholesome bread is a good way to use leftover squash as well as to sample an interesting and hearty bread. Acorn squash is good but other varieties will work well too.

1 cup (250 ml) sugar
1/2 cup (125 ml) firmly-packed
   brown sugar
1 cup (250 ml) mashed cooked squash
1/2 cup (125 ml) oil
2 eggs
1/4 cup (50 ml) water
2 cups (500 ml) all-purpose flour

1 teaspoon (5 ml) baking soda
1/2 teaspoon (2 ml) salt
1/2 teaspoon (2 ml) ground nutmeg
1/2 teaspoon (2 ml) cinnamon
1/4 teaspoon (1 ml) ground ginger
2/3 cup (175 ml) chopped pecans
1 cup (250 ml) raisins

Assemble Mixer. In large mixer bowl combine sugar, brown sugar, squash, oil and eggs. Beat at #4 until well blended. Stir in water. Mix together the flour, baking soda, salt, nutmeg, cinnamon and ginger. Add to squash mixture, and mix well. Assemble Blender and blender-chop pecans. Stir in raisins and pecans. Turn batter into well-greased 9 x 5 x 3-inch (23 x 13 x 8 cm) loaf pan. Bake at 350° F. (180° C.) for about 65 minutes, or until bread is done. Remove from pan; cool on rack. Wrap tightly and store overnight for easy slicing.
Yield: 1 loaf

CARROT BREAD

Carrots combined with raisins and nuts make this a delicious tea bread.

1 cup (250 ml) sugar
1/4 cup (50 ml) softened shortening
2 eggs
1 cup (250 ml) grated raw carrots
Grated rind of 1 medium orange
1-1/2 cups (375 ml) sifted all-purpose flour

2 teaspoons (10 ml) baking powder
1/4 teaspoon (1 ml) baking soda
1/2 teaspoon (2 ml) salt
1 cup (250 ml) golden raisins
1/2 cup (125 ml) chopped nuts

Assemble Mixer. Cream sugar with shortening in large mixer bowl at #4. Beat in eggs. Add orange rind and grated carrots. Sift flour with baking powder, baking soda and salt. Combine with the raisins and nuts; then add to the sugar mixture. Do not beat, but combine enough just to moisten all ingredients. Turn into a greased 9 x 5 x 3-inch (23 x 13 x 8 cm) loaf pan. Bake at 350° F. (180° C.) for about 55 minutes, or until bread tests done. Let cool in pan for 10 minutes; then turn onto wire rack. Cool completely before slicing.
Yield: 1 loaf.

PINEAPPLE COFFEE BREAD

2 cups (500 ml) sifted all-purpose flour
3/4 cup (200 ml) sugar
3 teaspoons (15 ml) baking powder
1 teaspoon (5 ml) salt
1/4 cup (50 ml) shortening

1 egg
1/2 cup (125 ml) undrained
　　crushed pineapple
1/2 cup (125 ml) milk

Sift flour with sugar, baking powder and salt. Cut in shortening well. Assemble Mixer. In small mixer bowl beat egg at #4 with pineapple and milk. Stir into flour mixture combining thoroughly. Spread into a greased 9-inch (23 cm) square pan. Sprinkle with Nut Topping. Bake at 350° F. (180° C.) for 40-45 minutes. Cut into squares and serve warm.

Nut Topping

1/2 cup (125 ml) whole almonds
1/2 cup (125 ml) firmly packed
　　dark brown sugar

1/4 cup (50 ml) all-purpose flour
3 tablespoons (45 ml) butter or margarine,
　　softened

Assemble Blender. Blender-grind almonds fine. Mix brown sugar and flour; then cut in butter. Mix with almonds.
Yield: 8 servings

CRANBERRY WHOLE WHEAT BREAD

1 cup (250 ml) walnuts
Grated rind of 1 orange
3/4 cup (200 ml) firmly packed
    light brown sugar
2 tablespoons (30 ml) vegetable
    shortening
1 egg

1-1/2 cups (375 ml) milk
2 cups (500 ml) whole wheat flour
1 cup (250 ml) all-purpose flour
3-1/2 teaspoons (17 ml) baking powder
1 teaspoon (5 ml) salt
1 can (8 ounces or 227 g) jellied
    cranberry sauce

Preheat oven to 350° F. (180° C.). Assemble Blender. Blender-chop walnuts. Set aside. Empty onto waxed paper. Blender-grind orange rind to desired consistency. Set aside. Assemble Mixer. Place light brown sugar, shortening and egg in large mixing bowl. Stir in the milk. Add dry ingredients, and mix at #3 until thoroughly blended. Cut jellied cranberry sauce into 1/2-inch (1 cm) cubes. Add to mixture along with orange rind and nuts. Fold to mix. Spread evenly into a greased and floured 9 x 5-inch (23 x 13 cm) loaf pan. Let stand at room temperature for 20 minutes. Bake for 1 hour. Unmold loaf, and cool completely on a wire rack before slicing into thin pieces.
Yield: 1 loaf

FRENCH BREAD

1 package (1/4 ounce or 7 g) active
    dry yeast
1/4 cup (50 ml) very warm water
1 cup (250 ml) boiling water
1 tablespoon (15 ml) shortening
2 teaspoons (10 ml) salt

1 tablespoon (15 ml) sugar
3/4 cup (200 ml) cold water
6 cups (1500 ml) sifted all-purpose
    flour
1 egg white, beaten

Preheat over to 425° F. (220° C.). Sprinkle dry yeast into very warm water (about 110° F. or 40° C.). Let stand for a few minutes. Then stir until dissolved. Assemble Doughmaker. Pour boiling water, over shortening, salt and sugar in large mixer bowl. Add cold water and cool to lukewarm. Add yeast. Gradually add enough flour to make stiff dough. Knead with doughmaker until smooth and satiny, about 4 minutes. Put in greased bowl; turn once. Cover and let rise until doubled, about 1-1/2 hours. Shape into two oblong loaves, about 14-inches (35 cm) long. Put on greased cookie sheets. Cover and let rise until doubled, about 1 hour. Brush with beaten egg white and with knife make 3 slashes across top. Bake for 30 minutes. Reduce heat to 350° F. (180° C.) and bake for 20 minutes more.
Yield: 2 loaves

FRENCH DINNER ROLLS

2 egg whites
3/4 cup (200 ml) hot water
1 tablespoon (15 ml) sugar
1 teaspoon (5 ml) salt
2 tablespoons (30 ml) butter

1 package (1/4 ounce or 7 g) active
   dry yeast
1/4 cup (50 ml) very warm water
4 cups (1000 ml) all-purpose flour
Cornmeal

Assemble Mixer. In small mixer bowl beat the egg whites at #10 until stiff. In large mixer bowl combine the hot water, sugar, salt and butter. Beat at #4 until the butter melts. Add yeast to 1/4 cup warm water, stirring to dissolve. Add the yeast mixture to half the flour. Assemble Doughmaker. Beat to make a soft but elastic dough. Fold in the beaten egg whites and the remaining flour. Knead with Dough-maker until smooth and elastic. Cover and let rise 2 hours. Punch down and let rise 1 hour. Turn the dough onto a lightly floured board and knead lightly. Divide into 18-24 pieces and let rest for 10 minutes. Shape the pieces into Parkerhouse-shaped rolls and place on buttered cookie sheet that has been sprinkled with cornmeal. Cover and let rise 45 minutes. Bake at 425° F. (220° C.) for 15-20 minutes.
Yield: 1-1/2 to 2 dozen

CHEESE DILL BREAD

This is an excellent recipe. Delicious toasted or for a ham sandwich.

1 package (1/4 ounce or 7 g) active
   dry yeast
1/4 cup (50 ml) warm water
1 cup (250 ml) cottage cheese
2 tablespoons (30 ml) sugar
1 tablespoon (15 ml) instant minced
   onion
2 teaspoons (10 ml) dill seed

1 tablespoon (15 ml) butter or margarine
1/2 teaspoon (2 ml) salt
1/2 teaspoon (2 ml) baking soda
1 egg
2-1/4 cups (550 ml) all-purpose flour
Butter, melted
Kosher salt

Dissolve yeast in warm water. In small saucepan, heat cheese to lukewarm. Assemble Doughmaker. In large mixer bowl, combine yeast, cheese, sugar, onion, dill seed, butter, salt, baking soda and egg. Mix at #10 until thoroughly blended. Add flour. Continue mixing. Cover and let rise until doubled in bulk, about 1-1/2 hours. Stir down dough; place in greased 1-1/2 quart (1.5 liter) round baking dish. Cover; let rise again until double in bulk, about 40 minutes. Bake at 350° F. (180° C.) for 45-50 minutes. Remove from dish, and brush top with butter; then sprinkle with a little salt for garnish.
Yield: 1 loaf

OATMEAL BREAD

2 packages (1/4 ounce or 7 g each)
   active dry yeast
1/2 cup (125 ml) very warm water
1-1/4 cups (300 ml) boiling water
1 cup (250 ml) quick-cooking
   rolled oats
1/2 cup (125 ml) molasses
1/3 cup (75 ml) shortening

1 tablespoon (15 ml) salt
6 to 6-1/4 cups (1500-1550 ml) sifted
   all-purpose flour
2 eggs, beaten
4 tablespoons (60 ml) rolled oats
1 egg white
1 tablespoon (15 ml) water
Rolled oats

Preheat oven to 375° F. (190° C.). Sprinkle dry yeast into very warm water. Assemble Doughmaker. In large mixer bowl combine boiling water, quick-cooking rolled oats, molasses, shortening and salt. Cool to lukewarm. Stir in two cups flour. Add beaten eggs and yeast. Beat well. Add enough remaining flour to make a soft dough. Turn out on lightly floured surface; cover and let rest 10 minutes. Knead until smooth. Place in lightly-greased bowl, turning dough once. Cover and let rise until doubled in bulk, about 1-1/2 hours. Punch down. Coat two well-greased 9 x 5 x 3-inch (23 x 13 x 8 cm) loaf pans with the rolled oats. Divide dough in half. Shape into loaves and place in pans. Cover. Let double in bulk, about 1 hour. Brush with mixture of the egg white and water. Sprinkle lightly with rolled oats. Bake for 1 hour and 10 minutes. Cover with foil, after baking 15 minutes, if tops are getting too brown.
Yield: 2 loaves

Chapter Three

SOUPS

CREAM OF SPINACH SOUP

1/4 cup (50 ml) boiling water
2 packages (10 ounces or 280 g each)
   frozen spinach
1/4 cup (50 ml) finely-chopped
   onion

1/4 cup (50 ml) butter
1/4 cup (50 ml) flour
4 cups (1 liter) milk
1 teaspoon (5 ml) salt
Croutons

Add boiling water to the spinach; let stand until spinach is heated through. Assemble Blender. Put spinach into blender container. Cover and process at BLEND. Empty container; then blender-chop onion. Brown onion in butter; stir in flour. Cook until bubbly; slowly add milk. Cook, stirring constantly, until thickened. Add spinach and salt. Let stand about 15 minutes. Serve garnished with croutons.
Yield: 6 servings

STRAWBERRY-BLUSH APPLE SOUP

This is a typically Scandinavian fruit soup, used both as a beginning course and as a dessert in those countries.

2 tablespoons (30 ml) fruit juice or
   water
2 apples, cut in eighths
2 tablespoons (30 ml) sugar
1-1/2 cups (375 ml) water
1/2 cup (125 ml) sugar
1 stick cinnamon

3 cups (750 ml) apple juice
1 cup (250 ml) pineapple juice
2 teaspoons (10 ml) lemon juice
3 tablespoons (45 ml) cornstarch
1/4 cup (50 ml) water
10 ounces (280 g) frozen strawberries

Assemble Blender. Put liquid and 4 or 5 pieces of apple into the blender container, cover and process at PUREE until smooth. Increase speed to BLEND, remove feeder cap and add remaining apples, a few at a time. Add the sugar. This will yield about 1 cup of applesauce. Now place applesauce, water and sugar in a saucepan with cinnamon stick, apple juice, pineapple juice and lemon juice. Simmer 10 minutes. Remove cinnamon stick. Mix cornstarch with water. Stir into fruit mixture in saucepan. Simmer 5 minutes, or until slightly thickened and clear. Stir in strawberries; they will thaw almost at once in the hot liquid. Chill well.
Yield: 8 servings

SWEDISH CABBAGE SOUP

1 large head cabbage, cored and
   cut into wedges
1/4 cup (50 ml) butter
3 tablespoons (45 ml) brown sugar

4 cups (1000 ml) beef bouillon
1 teaspoon (5 ml) salt
1/2 teaspoon (2 ml) pepper
1/4 teaspoon (1 ml) ground allspice

Assemble Salad Maker. Thin-slice cabbage. In a deep kettle brown cabbage in hot butter on all sides. The color should be light brown. Stir occasionally. Add sugar and cook, stirring until sugar is dissolved. Add beef bouillon, salt, pepper and allspice. Simmer, covered, for about 1 hour.
Yield: 6-8 servings

CREAM OF CAULIFLOWER SOUP

1 medium cauliflower, separated
   into flowerets
Water
4 cups (1 liter) milk

2 tablespoons (30 ml) butter
2 tablespoons (30 ml) all-purpose flour
Salt and pepper
1 raw carrot

Put cauliflower in a pan with water to cover and cook until tender. Drain. Assemble Blender. Put half the milk, butter, the flour, seasoning and half the cauliflower into the blender. Cover and process until pureed. Empty into saucepan. Repeat blending of remaining milk and cauliflower. Add to pan and heat thoroughly, stirring continuously. Assemble Salad Maker. Use Grating Disc to grate the carrot. Serve with grated carrot sprinkled on top.
Yield: 6-8 servings

CUCUMBER YOGURT SOUP

1 medium cucumber, peeled, seeded
   and cut into 1-inch pieces
1 cup (250 ml) chicken broth
1 cup (250 ml) plain yogurt

1/2 clove garlic, minced
Salt and pepper to taste
Mint

Assemble Blender. Put all ingredients, except mint, in the blender container. Cover and process at PUREE, increasing speed if necessary. Chill well. Stir and serve with mint sprinkled on top.
Yield: 4-6 servings

ITALIAN MINESTRONE

In Italy anything containing a starch such as noodles or rice is called "minestra"; hence, the name minestrone soup. This recipe is heartier than the usual one because of the addition of fish pieces.

1 medium onion
1 medium carrot
2 stalks celery
1/4 cup (50 ml) salad oil
2 cups (500 ml) clam juice
2 cups (500 ml) water
1 can (2 pounds 3 ounces or 992 g)
   Italian tomatoes

2 cups (500 ml) thin noodles, uncooked
1/2 teaspoon (2 ml) oregano
1/2 teaspoon (2 ml) Italian seasoning
1/2 teaspoon (2 ml) garlic powder
Salt and pepper
2 pounds (1 kg) fish fillets
Grated Parmesan cheese, optional

Assemble Blender. Water-chop onion, carrot and celery. Saute in salad oil until vegetables are tender. Add clam juice, water, tomatoes, noodles and seasonings. Simmer, covered, 30 minutes. Cut fish into bite-size pieces. Add to soup and simmer until fish flakes easily when tested with a fork, about 10 minutes. Serve with grated Parmesan cheese, if desired.
Yield: 6 servings

POTAGE CRECY

For people who don't like carrots, this soup will be an exciting discovery. It's a wonderful new way to treat a rather common vegetable.

1 pound (454 g) carrots, peeled and
   cut into 1-inch pieces
1 small onion, quartered
1 medium potato, peeled and cut
   into 1-inch pieces
3 tablespoons (45 ml) butter

1/2 teaspoon (2 ml) salt
Pepper
1/2 teaspoon (2 ml) sugar
3 cups (750 ml) beef consomme
1 tablespoon (15 ml) chopped parsley
1 teaspoon (5 ml) marjoram

Assemble Blender. Blender water-chop carrots, onion and potato. Drain liquid. Melt butter in a heavy saucepan. Add the vegetables. Season with salt, pepper and sugar. Cover and cook over low heat 15 minutes. Pour half the vegetables into blender container with half the consomme. Cover and process at PUREE. Repeat with remaining ingredients. Serve hot garnished with chopped parsley and marjoram.
Yield: 4 servings

HUNGARIAN TOMATO SOUP

Soups play an important role in the eating habits of the Hungarian family. Hearty soups are perfect for cold weather, but when the garden is in bloom, cold fruit soups and vegetable soups are favorites.

2 pounds (1 kg) ripe tomatoes
1/2 cup (125 ml) chopped onion
1 2-inch (5 cm) strip lemon peel
Sprig parsley
2 teaspoons (10 ml) paprika (Hungarian sweet red paprika is best)
1-1/2 tablespoons (22 ml) sugar

1 teaspoon (5 ml) salt, or to taste
2 cups (500 ml) dry white wine
Lemon juice, to taste
Sour cream
Paprika
Lemon wedges

Drop tomatoes in boiling water one minute. Peel under running cold water. Combine tomatoes with onion, lemon peel, parsley, paprika, sugar, salt and white wine. Cook gently until tomatoes are soft, about 15 minutes. Place in blender container. Cover and process at PUREE until smooth. Add lemon juice, depending on tartness of tomatoes. Chill well. Serve icy cold garnished with a dollop of sour cream, a dash of paprika and lemon wedge.
Yield: 4-6 servings

ONION SOUP

If there is one French dish which is popular all over the world, it is onion soup.

6 medium onions
1/4 cup (50 ml) butter
4 cans (10-1/2 ounces or 28 g each) condensed beef consomme, undiluted

1 teaspoon (5 ml) salt
4-6 slices French bread, 1-inch (2.5 cm) thick
Parmesan cheese, grated

Assemble Salad Maker. Thin-slice onions. Heat butter in large skillet. Add onion; saute, stirring, until golden, about 8 minutes. Combine onion, beef consomme and salt in a saucepan. Bring to boiling. Reduce heat and simmer, covered, 30 minutes. Meanwhile, toast bread slices. Sprinkle one side of each piece with some grated Parmesan cheese. Put under broiler 1 minute, or until cheese is bubbly. To serve, pour soup into individual soup bowls. Float toasted bread, cheese side up, on soup. Sprinkle grated cheese on top.
Yield: 4-6 servings

CHILLED AVOCADO SOUP

This soup is a quick and easy recipe. Very refreshing for a summer luncheon.

1 can (10-1/2 ounces or 280 g) condensed beef consomme, undiluted
1 large ripe avocado, peeled, seeded
   and cut into 1-inch pieces
1/4 cup (50 ml) cold water
1 teaspoon (5 ml) salt

2 teaspoons (10 ml) grated lemon peel
2 tablespoons (30 ml) lemon juice
1 cup (250 ml) sour cream
1 pint (0.5 liter) fresh oysters
Parsley
Lemon wedges

Assemble Blender. Put consomme and avocado into blender container with water, salt, lemon peel and lemon juice. Cover and process at BLEND until smooth. Add sour cream blending until smooth. Chill thoroughly. Rinse oysters in cold water and drain well. To serve, pour into chilled dishes; add 2 or 3 raw oysters per serving. Sprinkle with parsley and garnish with lemon wedges. This soup must be served ice cold.

Yield: 4 generous servings

VEGETABLE SOUP

3 potatoes, peeled
2 purple-top turnips, peeled
3 carrots
2 stalks celery
Half a small head of cabbage

1 cup (250 ml) green beans
10 cups (2.5 liters) chicken stock
5 peppercorns
1 cup (250 ml) peas
Herb Butter

Assemble Salad Maker. Cut the potatoes, turnips, carrots and celery with French Fry Cutter. Change blade to Shredder Disc and shred cabbage. Cut beans into 1-inch (2.5 cm) pieces. In large pot, combine chicken stock with potatoes, turnips, carrots, celery, cabbage and peppercorns. Bring to a boil. Lower heat. Cover and simmer about 1-1/2 hours. Add beans and peas. Simmer about 10 minutes. If using frozen beans and peas, add them last, just to heat well. Spoon into serving bowls. Pass Herb Butter separately so guests may put a spoonful into soup.

Herb Butter

4 tablespoons (60 ml) butter,
   softened
2 tablespoons (30 ml) parsley

2 teaspoons (10 ml) chives
1 teaspoon (5 ml) garlic powder

Combine all ingredients together. Serve in small bowl.

Yield: 10 servings

POTATO SPINACH SOUP

2-3 medium potatoes, cooked and
    quartered
1/3 medium onion
2 tablespoons (30 ml) butter
1 cup (250 ml) water
2 chicken bouillon cubes
1 teaspoon (5 ml) salt

1/2 teaspoon (2 ml) grated lemon peel
1/2 pound (227 g) fresh spinach
2 cups (500 ml) milk
1/4 cup (50 ml) lemon juice
1 cup (250 ml) sour cream
Grated fresh lemon peel, optional

In a large saucepan, put onion, butter, water, bouillon cubes, salt, lemon peel. Cover; bring to a boil. Simmer to cook onion slightly. Add potatoes and spinach and simmer 5 additional minutes. Assemble Blender. Put half the mixture into blender container. Set blender cover ajar to let steam escape and process at PUREE. Empty into large mixing bowl. Repeat with remaining half of cooked mixture. Assemble Mixer. Add milk, lemon juice and sour cream, and thoroughly mix at low speed. Chill several hours or overnight. Garnish with grated lemon peel or a thin slice of lemon.
Yield: 6 servings

YELLOW PEA SOUP

This robust soup is almost a meal in itself. The Polish sausage gives it a lively flavor.

1 pound (454 g) yellow split peas
2 pounds (1 kg) pork butt or smoked
    butt
8 cups (2 liters) water
2 teaspoons (10 ml) salt
1/2 teaspoon (2 ml) black pepper
2 teaspoons garlic salt or 1 clove
    garlic

1 bay leaf
1 teaspoon (5 ml) thyme
3 stalks celery
3 large carrots, pared
2 onions
4 medium potatoes, pared
1 pound Kielbasa sausage cut in
    1/2-inch circle*

In a large Dutch oven place peas, pork butt, water and seasonings. Simmer for 1-1/2 hours. Meanwhile, assemble Blender with Thick Slicing Disc. Slice celery, carrots, onions and potatoes. One hour before serving remove pork butt and add vegetables and sausage. Cut pork butt into cubes and return to soup. Simmer until vegetables are tender. Remove bay leaf before serving.
Yield: 8-10 servings

See Kielbasa sausage recipe on page 140.

SUMMER SQUASH SOUP

Robust and filling, this unique vegetable soup makes a perfect light lunch.

3 medium yellow squash
2 tablespoons (30 ml) butter
1-1/2 teaspoons (7 ml) garlic salt
1/2 teaspoon (2 ml) salt
1/4 teaspoon (1 ml) pepper

1/2 teaspoon (2 ml) rosemary
3 cups (750 ml) chicken broth
1 can (6 ounces or 168 g) boned chicken,
  flaked

Wash squash, but do not peel. Cut 12 paper-thin slices from the narrow ends and place slices in cold water to crisp. Reserve these slices for garnish. Cut remainder of squash into small chunks to make 5 or 6 cups. Saute very slowly in butter seasoned with garlic salt, salt, pepper and rosemary. Keep pan tightly covered and do not allow squash to brown. Add a few tablespoons water, if necessary, when squash is softened. Assemble Blender. Put 1 cup chicken broth and squash mixture into blender container. Cover and process at PUREE, increasing speed as necessary. Return puree to pan and add additional chicken broth and boned chicken. Heat until all flavors are well blended. Pour into serving dish or soup bowls and garnish with crisp squash slices.
Yield: 6 servings

CREAM OF POTATO SOUP

Long after other European countries had accepted the potato for human consumption, it was disdained in France. A soldier named Antoine Parmentier acquired a taste for it while he was a prisoner of war in Germany. In 1779 he entered it in an agricultural contest and won. To this day, cream of potato soup is Potage Parmentier in France.

1 medium onion, peeled and cubed
2/3 cup (175 ml) water
1 cup (250 ml) seasoned mashed
  potatoes
2 cups (500 ml) milk
1/4 cup (50 ml) heavy cream

1 tablespoon (15 ml) butter or
  margarine
1 chicken bouillon cube
Salt and pepper to taste
Parmesan cheese, grated
Parsley sprigs

Cook onion in water, covered, until it is tender. Remove from heat, and stir in mashed potatoes. Assemble Blender. Put mixture into blender container and process at PUREE until smooth. Put in saucepan with milk, heavy cream, butter and bouillon cube. Heat until very hot, but do not boil. Season to taste with salt and pepper. Serve with Parmesan cheese sprinkled over each portion and garnished with parsley sprigs.
Yield: 4 servings

Chapter Four

SALADS
AND
DRESSINGS

SAUERKRAUT SALAD

1 medium green pepper, cubed
1 large onion
4 cups (1000 ml) sauerkraut,
   drained

2 ounces (56 g) pimiento
1/2 cup (125 ml) honey
1/2 cup (125 ml) vinegar
1/2 cup (125 ml) salad oil

Assemble Blender. Blender chop green pepper. Assemble Salad Maker. Thin-slice onion at #8. Combine with sauerkraut. Assemble Blender. Put pimiento, honey, vinegar and salad oil in blender container. Cover and blender-chop. Add to sauerkraut mixture, tossing lightly. Refrigerate for several hours.
Yield: 10-15 servings

GINGER FRUIT SALAD

The combination of citrus fruits and ginger give this salad a unique flavor.

1 package (3 ounces or 84 g) orange
   gelatin
1/4 teaspoon (1 ml) ground ginger
Dash salt
1 cup (250 ml) boiling water

1 bottle (6 ounces or 168 g) ginger ale
3/4 cup (200 ml) fresh orange sections,
   halved
3/4 cup (200 ml) fresh grapefruit sections,
   halved

Dissolve orange gelatin, ground ginger and salt in boiling water. Add ginger ale. Place small mixer bowl filled with one cup of gelatin mixture into large mixer bowl of ice and water; stir until slightly thickened. Assemble Mixer. Whip at #9 until mixture is fluffy and thick. Pour into an 8-inch (20 cm) square pan. Chill until set, but not firm. Chill remaining gelatin until thickened, and fold in orange and grapefruit sections. Spoon this mixture gently over set gelatin. Chill until firm, about 4 hours. Cut into squares.
Yield: 6-8 servings

HUNGARIAN CUCUMBER SALAD

2 medium cucumbers, pared
2 teaspoons (10 ml) salt
3 tablespoons (45 ml) vinegar
3 tablespoons (45 ml) cold water
1/2 teaspoon (2 ml) sugar

1/2 teaspoon (2 ml) paprika
1/4 teaspoon (1 ml) pepper
1 clove garlic, minced
1 cup (250 ml) sour cream

Assemble Salad Maker. Thin-slice cucumbers at #6. Sprinkle with salt. Mix; chill for 1 hour. Assemble Blender. Put in remaining ingredients and half the paprika. Cover and process at MIX until well blended. Drain cucumbers; squeeze out water gently. Return cucumbers to bowl. Pour sauce over top. Toss lightly. Sprinkle remaining paprika over salad. Chill 1 to 2 hours.
Yield: 4-6 servings

WILTED GREENS

Choose a variety of textures for the salad greens in this salad. You may want to combine crisp iceberg lettuce, soft bibb lettuce, and crunchy romaine or escarole.

1 large head lettuce, cut into eighths
2 green onions cut in pieces
1 teaspoon (5 ml) salt
1 teaspoon (5 ml) pepper
1/4 cup (50 ml) vinegar

2 tablespoons (30 ml) water
2 teaspoons (10 ml) sugar
4 slices bacon, cut into pieces
1 hard-cooked egg, chopped

Assemble the Salad Maker. Shred lettuce into a large bowl using Thick Slicing Disc. Put remaining ingredients except egg and bacon into Mini-Blend jar and blender-chop onions. Fry bacon pieces until crisp. Add vinegar mixture to frying pan, and heat. Pour over tossed greens. Sprinkle with chopped egg.
Yield: 4 servings

ZUCCHINI SALAD

2 large zucchini, julienne sliced
2/3 cup (150 ml) salad oil
1/3 cup (75 ml) wine vinegar
1 clove garlic, minced
1 teaspoon (5 ml) sugar

1/2 teaspoon (2 ml) salt
Dash pepper
8 cups (2000 ml) salad greens, chilled
1/2 medium red onion
1 cup (250 ml) seasoned croutons

Assemble Salad Maker. Cut the zucchini with French Fry Cutter. Set aside. Use the Thin Slicing Disc to slice the red onion. Assemble Blender. Put salad oil, wine vinegar, garlic, sugar, salt and pepper in blender container. Cover and process at MIX. Combine with zucchini and chill to blend flavors. Toss before combining with salad greens, onion rings and croutons.
Yield: 8 servings

SOUTHERN SLAW

Coleslaw is usually considered a southern dish, but its origin is probably in the Dutch New Amsterdam (New York) gardens. The Dutch word for salad is sla, a word quickly adapted into the American vocabulary.

1 large head cabbage cut into wedges
1 medium onion, quartered
1 medium green pepper, seeded and
    quartered
1 cup plus 2 tablespoons (280 ml)
    sugar

3/4 cup (200 ml) salad oil
1 cup (250 ml) vinegar
1 teaspoon (5 ml) salt
1 teaspoon (5 ml) dry mustard
1 teaspoon (5 ml) celery seed

Assemble Salad Maker. Use Thin Slicing Disc for cabbage and onion. Use French Fry Cutter to dice pepper. Stir in 1 cup sugar. Put salad oil, vinegar, remaining sugar, salt, dry mustard and celery seed in a saucepan and bring to a boil. Pour over cabbage mixture; cool. Refrigerate until ready to serve.
Yield: 8-12 servings

WHIPPED CRANBERRY SALAD

A good accompaniment to chicken or turkey.

1 pound (454 g) cranberries
2 cups (500 ml) sugar
2 cups (500 ml) crushed pineapple,
    drained

30 miniature marshmallows
2 cups (500 ml) heavy cream
1/2 cup (125 ml) chopped walnuts

Assemble Food Grinder with Fine Disc. Grind cranberries. Add sugar, pineapple and marshmallows. Mix well. Refrigerate for several hours. Assemble Mixer. In small mixer bowl, whip heavy cream at #9. Fold whipped cream into cranberry mixture; add walnuts. Chill 4-5 hours.
Yield: 15-20 servings

CAULIFLOWER SALAD

1 medium cauliflower, separated
    into flowerets
2/3 cup (150 ml) salad oil
1/4 cup (50 ml) vinegar
1/3 cup (75 ml) stuffed green olives
1 green onion cut in pieces

1 tablespoon (15 ml) pickle relish
1 teaspoon (5 ml) salt
1 teaspoon (5 ml) paprika
Dash pepper
Tomato wedges

Cook cauliflower, covered, in small amount of boiling water for about 10 minutes, or until crispy tender. Drain. Place in shallow dish. Assemble Blender. Combine remaining ingredients, except tomato wedges, in blender container. Cover and blender-chop onions and olives. Pour over cauliflower. Chill for 3 hours. Drain. Serve garnished with tomato wedges.
Yield: 8-10 servings

SEA FOAM SALAD

Lime gelatin and delicate flavoring makes this an extra special treat. Serve with fresh fruits, if desired.

1 can (1 pound 14 ounces or 742 g) pear halves
1 package (3 ounces or 84 g) lime gelatin

6 ounces (168 g) cream cheese
2 tablespoons (30 ml) milk
1/2 cup (125 ml) heavy cream

Drain pear halves, reserving 1 cup of syrup. Assemble Blender. Blender-chop pears. Heat syrup to boiling. Pour over lime gelatin, and stir until gelatin is dissolved. Assemble Mixer. In large mixer bowl, beat cream cheese with milk at #4 until smooth. Gradually beat in hot gelatin. Chill until slightly thickened. Fold in pears. Meanwhile, in small mixer bowl, whip heavy cream at #9. Fold in whipped cream. Turn into 1-1/2 quart (1.5 liter) mold and chill until firm.
Yield: 8 servings

OLD-FASHIONED TOMATO SALAD

Perfectly seasoned tomatoes. Right with any meal, especially if they're fresh from the garden.

6 ripe tomatoes, chilled
3 tablespoons (45 ml) red wine vinegar
1/2 cup (125 ml) olive oil
2 teaspoons (10 ml) salt
1 teaspoon (5 ml) black pepper
Dash dry mustard

2 tablespoons (30 ml) chopped fresh chives
2 tablespoons (30 ml) chopped fresh parsley
1/2 teaspoon (2 ml) basil or 2 tablespoons (30 ml) chopped fresh sweet basil

Wash and dry chilled tomatoes. Slice thin, and arrange neatly on a serving platter. Assemble Blender. Put red wine vinegar, olive oil, salt, pepper and dry mustard in blender container. Cover and process at MIX until well combined. Pour over tomatoes. Sprinkle chopped chives, parsley and basil over tomatoes.
Yield: 6 servings

FRENCH COUNTRY-STYLE CUCUMBER SALAD

3 medium cucumbers, peeled and
    thin-sliced
1-1/2 teaspoons (7 ml) salt
3 tablespoons (45 ml) olive oil

1 teaspoon (5 ml) dill
Dash pepper
3 tablespoons (45 ml) lemon juice

Assemble Salad Maker. Slice cucumbers as indicated above. Sprinkle salt over cucumber slices, and let stand 20 minutes. Assemble Blender. Place olive oil, dill, pepper and lemon juice in blender container. Cover and process at WHIP until well blended. Drain liquid from cucumbers; pat slices dry with paper towel. Pour dressing over cucumbers. Toss lightly to coat slices. Chill before serving.
Yield: 6 servings

CHERRY MOLD

2 packages (3 ounces or 84 g each)
    cherry gelatin
2 cups (500 ml) boiling water
1 can (20 ounces or 560 g) cherry
    pie filling

1/3 cup (75 ml) claret wine
2 tablespoons (30 ml) lemon juice
1 package (3 ounces or 84 g) cream cheese
1 cup (250 ml) evaporated milk

Assemble Blender. Put cherry gelatin and boiling water into blender container. Cover and process at BEAT until dissolved. Pour into bowl, and add pie filling, claret wine and lemon juice. Assemble Mixer. In small mixer bowl beat cream cheese at #4 until light and fluffy. Add evaporated milk gradually to cream cheese. Blend with gelatin mixture. Chill until partly set. Stir mixture until cherries are evenly distributed. Turn into an 11 x 7 x 2-inch (27.5 x 18 x 5 cm) pan or individual molds. Chill until firm.
Yield: 8 servings

CABBAGE SALAD

1 medium head of cabbage, cut
   in wedges
1 carrot
2 tablespoons (30 ml) pimiento
2/3 cup (175 ml) pecans
3 slices pineapple, cut into chunks

1/2 cup (125 ml) mayonnaise
2 tablespoons (30 ml) olive oil
2 tablespoons (30 ml) vinegar or
   lemon juice
Salt and pepper
Dash hot pepper sauce

Assemble Salad Maker with Thin Slicing Disc. Slice cabbage. With Shredding Disc, process carrot. Assemble Blender. Blender-chop pimiento and pecans. Combine all ingredients. Chill.
Yield: 4-6 servings

MARINATED CELERY

1 bunch celery, cleaned and trimmed
2 tablespoons (30 ml) oil
2 tablespoons (30 ml) vinegar
1/2 cup (125 ml) white wine
A wedge of onion
1 teaspoon (5 ml) salt

1 teaspoon (5 ml) parsley
1/4 teaspoon (1 ml) thyme
1/2 cup (125 ml) water
Dash hot pepper sauce
Dash pepper

Assemble Salad Maker with the Thick Slicing Disc. Slice celery making about 5 cups (1250 ml). Set aside. Assemble Blender. Put remaining ingredients into blender container. Cover and process at LIQUEFY until thoroughly blended. Pour into saucepan; add celery. Cover and boil until tender, about 20 minutes. Pour into glass jar, pressing down celery so marinade covers it. Cover and keep in refrigerator. It will last for weeks. Add to tossed green salad or use as a relish with meat or fish.
Yield: 8-10 servings

MOLDED CRANBERRY RELISH

1-1/2 cups (375 ml) fresh cranberries
1 package (3 ounces or 84 g)
   raspberry gelatin
1/4 teaspoon (1 ml) ground nutmeg

1 cup (250 ml) boiling water
1 cup (250 ml) pineapple juice
3/4 cup (200 ml) diced celery
1/3 cup (75 ml) slivered almonds

Assemble Food Grinder with Coarse Disc. Grind the cranberries. Mix the raspberry gelatin and nutmeg together. Add boiling water. Stir until dissolved. Add pineapple juice. Chill until thickened. Assemble Salad Maker. Dice celery using the French Fry Cutter. Stir into mixture with slivered almonds. Pour into 5-cup (1250 ml) mold or small individual molds. Chill until firm. Unmold to serve.
Yield: 8-10 servings

ORANGE PERFECT SALAD

Fresh oranges add zest and color to this delicious gelatin salad. The recipe may be easily doubled and served for a large buffet dinner.

2 packages (3 ounces or 84 g each)
   orange gelatin
2 cups (500 ml) boiling water
1-1/2 cups (375 ml) orange juice
2 large oranges, peeled, sectioned,
   seeded and cut into bite-size pieces

1/4 cup (50 ml) pecans
1/4 cup (50 ml) sour cream
Lettuce cups

Dissolve orange gelatin completely in boiling water; add orange juice. Chill until thick and syrupy, but not set. Drain orange pieces well. Combine with about 2-1/4 cups (550 ml) thickened gelatin. Pour into an 8 x 8-inch (20 x 20 cm) pan or eight individual molds. Chill. Assemble Blender. Put remaining gelatin, sour cream and pecans into blender container. Cover and process at BLEND to thoroughly mix all ingredients. Pour sour cream mixture over the top of orange gelatin layer. Chill until firm; cut into squares, or unmold and serve on lettuce cups.
Yield: 8 servings

TWO-TONE CABBAGE SALAD

Slicing cabbage is no work at all with your food processor. The combination of red and green cabbage makes this a pretty dish.

1/4 medium head red cabbage
1/2 medium head green cabbage
1 egg yolk
1/2 teaspoon (2 ml) salt
1/2 teaspoon (2 ml) powdered mustard

Dash cayenne pepper
2 tablespoons (30 ml) cider vinegar
3/4 cup (200 ml) evaporated milk
4 lettuce leaves

Assemble Salad Maker with Thin Slicer and slice cabbage. Keep the two colors separate. Assemble Blender. Beat egg yolk at MIX; add salt, mustard, cayenne and vinegar. Gradually add milk. Add half of mixture to cabbage of each color and mix lightly. Put red cabbage mixture on lettuce leaf and top with green cabbage mixture.
Yield: 4 servings

HOT POTATO SALAD

4 large potatoes, peeled
1 large onion, cut in pieces
3 eggs
1/2 cup (125 ml) sugar
1/4 cup (50 ml) vinegar
2 tablespoons (30 ml) all-purpose flour

Dash salt
1/4 cup (50 ml) cold water
1 cup (250 ml) hot water
3 stalks celery
6 hard-cooked eggs

Assemble Salad Maker. Thick-slice potatoes and onion at #8. Cook potatoes in salted water. Assemble Mixer. In a large mixer bowl combine eggs, sugar, vinegar, flour, salt and cold water. Beat at #4 until thoroughly mixed. Add hot water. Transfer to saucepan and cook until thick. Meanwhile, assemble Blender. Chop celery and hard-cooked eggs. Mix together with cooked potatoes and sliced onions. Pour hot dressing over potato mixture, and sprinkle with celery seed. Serve immediately.
Yield: 8-10 servings

DAIRY DRESSING

1 cup (250 ml) cottage cheese
1/4 cup (50 ml) chili sauce
1/4 cup (50 ml) milk
2 tablespoons (30 ml) vegetable oil
1 teaspoon (5 ml) paprika

1/2 teaspoon (2 ml) salt
1 stalk celery, cubed
1/2 medium green pepper, cubed
1 slice onion, 1/2-inch (1 cm) thick

Assemble Blender. Put cottage cheese, chili sauce, milk, vegetable oil, paprika and salt into blender container. Cover and process at WHIP until well blended. Stop blender and add remaining ingredients. Cover and process two cycles at GRATE.
Yield: 2-1/4 cups (550 ml)

OLD-FASHIONED TOMATO DRESSING

A zippy-flavored dressing. Good over lettuce.

1 can (8 ounces or 227 g) tomato
  sauce
1/2 cup (125 ml) cider vinegar
1 small onion, quartered
2 tablespoons (30 ml) light brown
  sugar

2 tablespoons (30 ml) Worcestershire
  sauce
1 teaspoon (5 ml) salt
1 teaspoon (5 ml) paprika
1/4 teaspoon (1 ml) pepper
1 cup (250 ml) vegetable oil

Assemble Blender. Combine all ingredients, except vegetable oil, in blender container. Cover and process at BLEND until smooth. Remove feeder cap and pour vegetable oil into mixture in a steady stream. Continue blending until thickened and smooth. Refrigerate several hours before serving.
Yield: 3 cups (750 ml)

MUSTARD SOUR CREAM DRESSING

2 tablespoons (30 ml) mild mustard
2 teaspoons (10 ml) sugar
1/2 teaspoon (2 ml) salt

1/2 cup (125 ml) sour cream
2 tablespoons (30 ml) malt or cider
   vinegar

    Assemble Blender. Put mustard, sugar and salt in Mini-Blend container. Cover and process at BLEND. Add sour cream and vinegar. Continue processing. Cover; chill. Serve over tossed salad greens.
Yield: 2/3 cup (175 ml)

CELERY SEED SALAD DRESSING

1 cup (250 ml) sugar
1/4 medium onion
2 teaspoons (10 ml) celery seed
2 teaspoons (10 ml) dry mustard

1-1/2 teaspoons (7 ml) salt
2 teaspoons (10 ml) paprika
1/2 cup (125 ml) vinegar
2 cups (500 ml) salad oil

    Assemble Blender. Blender-grate onion with sugar. Add celery seed, dry mustard, salt, paprika and vinegar in blender container. Cover and process at WHIP until well blended. Remove feeder cap, increase speed to BLEND, and pour in the salad oil in a slow, steady stream. If necessary, stop Blender and use rubber spatula to keep mixture around processing blades. Store in covered jar in refrigerator, and let stand at room temperature for a few hours before serving to allow flavors to blend.
Yield: 3 cups (750 ml)

LEMON MAYONNAISE

1 egg
1 teaspoon (5 ml) Dijon mustard
1/2 teaspoon (2 ml) salt

2 tablespoons (30 ml) fresh lemon juice
1 cup (250 ml) vegetable oil
1 tablespoon (15 ml) chopped parsley

Assemble Blender. Break egg into blender container. Add Dijon mustard, salt, lemon juice and 1/4 cup (50 ml) vegetable oil. Process at MIX. Remove feeder cap, and pour in the remaining oil in a steady stream. If necessary, STOP BLENDER; use rubber spatula to keep mixture around the processing blades. Stir in parsley; refrigerate.
Yield: 1-1/4 cups (300 ml)

GUACAMOLE DRESSING

1/2 cup (125 ml) sour cream
2 ripe avocados, peeled, seeded
    and quartered
1 teaspoon (5 ml) grated lemon peel

2 tablespoons (30 ml) lemon juice
1 thin slice of onion
1 teaspoon (5 ml) salt
Dash hot pepper sauce

Assemble Blender. Put sour cream and the pieces of one avocado, lemon peel, lemon juice and onion into blender container. Cover and process at BLEND. Remove feeder cap, and add remaining avocado. Cover and process at BLEND until smooth. Empty through the base of the container to get out all the dressing.
Yield: 2-1/2 cups (625 ml)

POPPY SEED DRESSING

1/2 cup (125 ml) sugar
1 teaspoon (5 ml) salt
1 teaspoon (5 ml) dry mustard
1/2 teaspoon (2 ml) fresh grated
  lemon peel

1/4 of small onion
1/3 cup (75 ml) lemon juice
3/4 cup (200 ml) salad oil
1 tablespoon (15 ml) poppy seeds

Assemble Blender. Place all ingredients in blender container, except poppy seeds. Cover and process at WHIP until well blended. Uncover and stir in poppy seeds. Chill. Serve with fresh fruits.
Yield: 1-1/2 cups (375 ml)

BLUE CHEESE OR ROQUEFORT DRESSING

1 cup (250 ml) evaporated milk,
  undiluted
1/2 cup (125 ml) salad oil
4 tablespoons (60 ml) vinegar

1/2 teaspoon (2 ml) salt
Dash of garlic powder
1/2 cup (125 ml) crumbled blue or
  Roquefort cheese

Assemble Blender. Put all ingredients except cheese into blender container, cover and process at MIX until smooth. Stop blender; add cheese, cover and process 1 cycle at BEAT. (If a smoother dressing is desired, put all ingredients into blender container, cover and process at MIX until smooth.)
Yield: 2 cups (500 ml)

Chapter Five
VEGETABLES

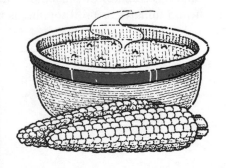

VEGETABLE STEW

3 medium onions
3 green peppers, quartered and
    seeded
3 tablespoons (45 ml) butter

3 tomatoes, peeled and diced or 1 can
    (1 pound or 454 g) tomatoes, drained
    and diced
1 (16 ounce of 454 g) can whole kernel
    corn
Salt and pepper

Assemble Salad Maker with Thick Slicer. Slice onions and green peppers. Saute onion in butter in saucepan. Add peppers. Add tomatoes. Bring to a boil; then simmer, covered, for 10 minutes. Add corn and simmer, covered for another 5 minutes. Season with salt and pepper to taste.
Yield: 6 servings

SWEET POTATO PUFFS

Easy to fix and delightful to look at, these puffs are excellent with meat or poultry.

3 large sweet potatoes
1/2 cup (125 ml) milk
1/2 teaspoon (2 ml) salt
1/2 cup (125 ml) butter or margarine

1/4 cup (50 ml) firmly packed light
    brown sugar
Dash pumpkin pie spice
1/4 cup (50 ml) blanched slivered almonds

Scrub sweet potatoes. Cut off ends and place in baking pan. Bake at 400° F. (200° C.) for 1 hour. Cut potatoes lengthwise into halves. Assemble Mixer. Scoop pulp into large mixer bowl. Add milk, salt and 1/4 cup (50 ml) of the butter. Beat at #4 until light and fluffy. Fill potato shells with mixture. Return to oven for 5 minutes. Meanwhile, in small mixer bowl, cream together at #4 the remaining butter, sugar and pumpkin pie spice. Fold in slivered almonds. Take potato shells out of oven and place dollop of the almond topping on each potato half. Return to oven and heat 5 minutes or until topping is melted.
Yield: 6 servings

BROCCOLI AMANDINE

This is a good way to serve leftover broccoli. The toasted almonds add a crunchy texture.

2-1/2 tablespoons (37 ml) all-
    purpose flour
1-1/4 cups (300 ml) milk
1/4 teaspoon (1 ml) salt
Dash cayenne pepper
4 tablespoons (60 ml) butter or
    margarine

2 egg yolks
2 tablespoons (30 ml) lemon juice
1-1/2 pounds (1.5 liters) cooked
    broccoli
1/3 cup (75 ml) toasted blanched
    slivered almonds*

Assemble Blender. Put flour, milk, salt, pepper and half the butter into blender container. Cover and process at MIX until well blended. Pour into saucepan and cook until thickened. Return to blender container; add remaining butter, egg yolks and lemon juice. Cover and process at BLEND. Return to heat. Cook, stirring constantly, about 5 minutes longer, but do not boil. Pour over hot cooked broccoli, and sprinkle with toasted slivered almonds.

Yield: 5-6 servings

To toast almonds, put almonds in flat pan in single layer. Toast, stirring often, at 300° F. (150° C.) for about 15 minutes, or until they begin to turn color. Do not wait for nuts to become golden brown. The heat in the nuts will continue to toast them out of the oven.

CELERY AMANDINE

1 bunch celery, thick sliced,
    reserving top leaves
1/2 cup (125 ml) cooking liquid
1 cup (250 ml) milk

4 tablespoons (60 ml) butter
1 teaspoon (5 ml) salt
1/4 cup (50 ml) flour
1/3 cup (75 ml) almonds or walnuts

Assemble Blender. Cook celery in 1 quart (1 liter) of boiling water for 10-12 minutes. Drain, reserving 1/2 cup (125 ml) of cooking liquid. In blender container, place milk, butter, salt and flour. Process at WHIP. Add celery tops and process 1 cycle at CHOP. Pour into a saucepan and add remaining cooking liquid. Heat until thick, stirring constantly. Put half of celery into a buttered 1-quart (1 liter) casserole. Pour over 1/2 the sauce. Repeat. In Mini-Blend container process the almonds 2 cycles at GRIND. Sprinkle over the top of casserole. Bake uncovered 30 minutes at 350° F. (180° C.).
Yield: 1 (1 quart or 1 liter) casserole

FRENCH PROVINCIAL POTATOES

Here is an unusual and hearty dish from the French provinces. Serve with chops and roasts.

Salted water
6 medium potatoes, peeled
6 slices bacon, diced
1 medium onion, cut into 1-inch
    pieces

3-4 sprigs parsley
8 eggs
1 teaspoon (5 ml) salt
1/4 teaspoon (1 ml) pepper
1/4 teaspoon (1 ml) paprika

In salted water to cover, bring potatoes to boiling. Boil gently, covered, until almost tender, about 20 minutes. Drain and cut into 1/8-inch (0.3 cm) thick slices. In heavy skillet, fry bacon until crisp; drain and reserve bacon drippings. Assemble Blender. Blender-chop onion and parsley. In 2 tablespoons bacon drippings, saute the chopped onion until golden. Add the potatoes, 1/3 at a time. Saute until browned; remove when brown. Add more drippings, if needed. Return all potatoes to skillet in layers making sure slices lie flat and sprinkling parsley between layers. Assemble Mixer. In small mixer bowl beat eggs with salt, pepper and paprika at #4 until well combined. Pour over potatoes. Sprinkle with crisp bacon. Cook, covered, over low heat about 5 minutes, or until eggs are set.
Yield: 6-8 servings

CAULIFLOWER IN CHEESE PUFF

An elegant way to dress up cauliflower.

1 large cauliflower
Salted water
1-1/2 cups (375 ml) medium
   white sauce*

1 cup Cheddar cheese, cubed
4 eggs separated
1 teaspoon sugar
Salt and pepper

Trim cauliflower and break into flowerets. Cook in boiling salted water until barely tender. Put in buttered shallow baking dish; reserve a few flowerets for garnish. Make a medium-thick white sauce.* Assemble Blender. Blender-grate Cheddar cheese. Add grated cheese to white sauce. Assemble Mixer. Beat egg yolks, sugar, salt and pepper to taste at #4; then add white sauce. In small mixer bowl beat egg whites at #10 until stiff, and fold into sauce. Pour over cauliflower. Bake at 350° F. (180° C.) for about 25 minutes, or until sauce is firm. Garnish with remaining flowerets.

Yield: 4-6 servings

* See White Sauce recipe on page 134.

EVERGREEN ZUCCHINI

The main work of slicing is easily done with your food processor, making this a simple recipe that tastes very good, and goes particularly well with chicken or turkey.

3-1/2 to 4 pounds (1.7-2 kg) zucchini,
   washed and ends removed
Water
1 tablespoon (15 ml) salt
A wedge of onion

1 cup (250 ml) fresh parsley
1/4 cup (50 ml) butter
1/2 teaspoon (2 ml) grated lemon peel
2 tablespoons (30 ml) lemon juice

Wash zucchini. Assemble Salad Maker with Thick Slicer. Slice zucchini at #6. Put an inch of water in a large frying pan and add zucchini and salt. Cover, bring to a boil and simmer about 8 minutes until tender, but still crisp. Drain well. While zucchini is cooking, assemble Blender and blender-chop parsley and onion together. Set aside. Heat butter, onion-parsley mixture, lemon peel and lemon juice until butter is melted. Pour over drained zucchini and toss thoroughly.

Yield: 8 servings

ASPARAGUS LYONNAISE

Here asparagus becomes a special chilled treat. Delicious with roasts.

2 pounds (1 kg) fresh asparagus or 2
    packages frozen asparagus tips
Boiling salted water
1/4 cup (50 ml) tarragon-flavored
    white wine vinegar

1/2 cup (125 ml) salad oil
2 teaspoons (10 ml) chervil
1/2 teaspoon (2 ml) salad herbs
1 teaspoon (5 ml) salt
Salad greens

Cut tough stem ends from fresh asparagus. Cook in boiling salted water until just tender. Drain and rinse with cold water at once to retain color. Assemble Blender. Combine wine vinegar, salad oil, chervil, salad herbs and salt in blender container. Cover and process at WHIP. Turn asparagus into shallow glass pan. Pour vinegar mixture over asparagus. Cover tightly and chill overnight. To serve, lift asparagus carefully onto salad greens arranged on chilled plates. Spoon some dressing over asparagus.
Yield: 8 servings

POTATO SOUFFLE

The secret of a good souffle is the folding of the egg whites. Mixing them will not allow the souffle to rise. So, fold by hand and you'll have a dish that looks pretty and tastes good.

4 cups (1000 ml) leftover mashed
    potatoes
2 teaspoons (10 ml) salt
1/2 cup (125 ml) grated Parmesan cheese

1/2 teaspoon (2 ml) ground nutmeg
2 cups (500 ml) light cream
6 eggs, separated

Assemble Mixer. In a large mixer bowl combine potatoes, salt, cheese, nutmeg and cream until well blended. Add egg yolks and beat until blended. Put mixture into another bowl, and wash mixer bowl. In large mixer bowl beat egg whites at #10 until stiff but not dry. Fold into potato mixture. Turn into an ungreased 2-1/2 to 3 quart (2-1/2 to 3 liters) souffle dish. Bake at 375° F. (190° C.) for 50-60 minutes, or until souffle is golden. Serve at once.
Yield: 8-10 servings

WILTED CABBAGE

This cabbage dish tastes much like sauerkraut, and would go well with corned beef or brisket.

1/3 medium-sized head red cabbage, cut in wedges
1/3 medium-sized head green cabbage, cut in wedges
4 slices bacon

1/2 cup (125 ml) cider vinegar
2 tablespoons (30 ml) sugar
1 teaspoon (5 ml) salt
Dash pepper
1/2 cup (125 ml) water

Assemble Salad Maker with Thin Slicer and slice cabbage. Keep both colors of cabbage separated. Fry bacon in skillet until crisp; remove. To fat in skillet, add vinegar, sugar, salt, pepper and water. Bring to boiling. Divide mixture, adding half to red and half to green cabbage. Cook quickly, about 5 minutes for green cabbage and 8 minutes for red cabbage. Serve in two-sectioned dish with crumbled bacon sprinkled over top.
Yield: 4 servings

ORIENTAL CARROTS

A wonderful sweet and sour flavor gives this recipe its unique taste. It's a good complement to any meat or poultry.

1 pound (454 g) fresh carrots, pared
1 can (8 ounces or 227 g) pineapple chunks in syrup
1 green pepper, quartered and seeded

1 small onion
1 tablespoon (15 ml) cornstarch
1 tablespoon (15 ml) soy sauce
1 tablespoon (15 ml) vinegar

Assemble Salad Maker with Thick Slicer. Slice carrots. Put into a skillet. Drain the pineapple chunks, reserving the syrup. Add water to make the syrup amount to 1 cup (250 ml) of liquid, and add to the carrots; cover and simmer 8 to 10 minutes, or until they are crisp-tender. While carrots cook, thick-slice the pepper and onion in the Salad Maker. Set aside. Blend the cornstarch, soy sauce and vinegar together and add the mixture with the sliced vegetables and pineapple chunks to the carrots. Stir quickly. Cook until sauce is thickened and shiny. Serve immediately.
Yield: 4-6 servings

ZUCCHINI ROMAN STYLE

16 small zucchini, washed and ends
    removed
1/4 cup (50 ml) olive oil
2 teaspoons (10 ml) salt

2 teaspoons (10 ml) oregano
1/4 teaspoon (1 ml) garlic powder
1/4 teaspoon (1 ml) black pepper
2 tablespoons (30 ml) parsley

Assemble Salad Maker with French Fry Cutter. Process the zucchini through it at #6. Heat oil in a large skillet. Saute zucchini until golden, sprinkling with salt, oregano, garlic powder and pepper. Blend together. Sprinkle parsley over top; turn heat to low and simmer for a few minutes. Zucchini should be crisp-tender. Serve at once.
Yield: 16 servings

PICKLED BEETS

1 onion
1/2 cup (125 ml) cider vinegar
1/4 cup (50 ml) sugar
1/2 teaspoon (1 ml) salt
1/2 teaspoon (1 ml) peppercorns

1 bay leaf, crumbled
1 can (16 ounces or 454 g) sliced beets
    with liquid reserved **or**
1 bunch fresh beets (about 5 or 7 small)

If fresh beets are being used, wash them, leaving 2 inches of stem on. Put them in a small amount of boiling water, cover and simmer slowly until they are tender. This will take about 30 minutes. Reserve half a cup of the cooking liquid. Plunge the cooked beets into cold water, and when they can be handled, slip the skins off, and trim off the stems. Assemble Salad Maker with Thin Slicing Disc. Slice onion. With French Fry Cutter cut fresh cooked beets. Assemble Blender. Put cider vinegar, sugar, salt, peppercorns, bay leaf, and half a cup of reserved beet liquid into blender container. Cover and process at WHIP. Combine sliced onion, vinegar mixture and beets in saucepan. Bring to a boil. Serve hot or cold.
Yield: 6 servings

ORANGE CARROTS

1 pound (454 g) carrots
3/4 cup (200 ml) water
1/2 teaspoon (2 ml) salt
1/2 teaspoon (2 ml) grated orange
   peel

1 medium orange, peeled and cut into
   bite-size pieces
2 tablespoons (30 ml) butter
1 tablespoon (15 ml) chives

Wash and scrape carrots. Assemble Salad Maker with the Thick Slicer. Slice carrots. Put carrots in saucepan, add water and bring to a boil. Add salt. Cook covered about 8 to 10 minutes until crisp-tender. Drain. Add orange peel and pieces of orange, butter and chives. Return to low heat. Stir gently until butter is melted and orange pieces are warm. Serve at once.
Yield: 4 servings

VEGETABLE RELISH

This colorful vegetable medley is a fine combination of many flavors. Its unusual tart flavor is especially good with a veal or chicken dish that is not highly seasoned.

1 green pepper
1 onion
1 bunch celery, cleaned and trimmed
1 can (16 ounces or 454 g) small
   peas, drained
1 can (8 ounces or 227 g) French-
   style green beans, drained

1 jar (4 ounces or 112 g) pimientos
1 cup (250 ml) vinegar
1 tablespoon (15 ml) salt
1 tablespoon (15 ml) celery seed
1/2 cup (125 ml) oil
1 teaspoon (5 ml) mustard seed

Assemble Salad Maker with the Thick Slicing Disc. Slice green pepper, onion and celery. Combine with peas and green beans. Assemble Blender. Blender-chop pimientos. Add vinegar, salt, celery seed, oil and mustard seed. Cover and process at WHIP. Pour over vegetables. Toss lightly and let stand in refrigerator overnight.
Yield: 6-8 servings

CORN PIE

An adaptation of a South American favorite, this corn recipe is unusual and delicious. The saltine crust is a complimentary flavor.

1-1/4 cups (300 ml) fine saltine
    cracker crumbs
1/2 cup (125 ml) melted butter
1-1/4 cups (300 ml) milk
2 cups (500 ml) fresh or frozen corn
1/4 teaspoon (1 ml) salt
Dash white pepper

2 tablespoons (30 ml) instant minced
    onion
2 tablespoons (30 ml) all-purpose
    flour
2 eggs, beaten
Paprika

Preheat oven to 400° F. (200° C.). Assemble Blender. Blender-crumb saltine crackers. Combine crumbs with melted butter. Set aside about half a cup of the mixture. With spoon, press remainder into 9-inch (23 cm) pie plate. Mix 1 cup milk, corn, salt, pepper and onion in saucepan. Bring to a boil; reduce heat, and simmer for 3 minutes. Blend flour and remaining milk. Stir into hot mixture, and cook, stirring until thickened. Cool slightly. Gradually add eggs, stirring well. Pour into lined pie shell and sprinkle with reserved crumbs and paprika. Bake for 15 minutes. Cut and serve hot.
Yield: 8 servings

Chapter Six
MAIN DISHES

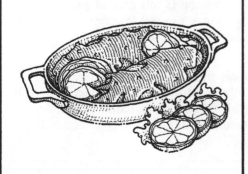

LAMB CHEESE PIE

1 onion wedge
1-1/2 cups (375 ml) Cheddar cheese
   cubes
1 pound (454 g) ground lamb
4 eggs, slightly beaten

1/2 cup (125 ml) milk
1 teaspoon (5 ml) salt
1/4 teaspoon (1 ml) pepper
1 8-inch (20 cm) pie shell, unbaked
2 tablespoons (30 ml) chopped parsley

Assemble Blender. Blender-grate onion and cheese; set aside. Cook ground lamb over low heat until browned, stirring occasionally. Drain off drippings. Combine lamb, onion, eggs, 1 cup grated Cheddar cheese, milk, salt and pepper. Mix well. Turn into pricked pastry shell. Top with remaining Cheddar cheese and parsley. Bake at 400° F. (200° C.) for 40 minutes or until set.
Yield: 4 servings

PLUM DUCKLING

This piquant plum sauce makes the duckling a superb Oriental facsimile of the famous Peking dish. Serve it hot or cold.

1 4-5 pound (2-2.5 kg) duckling
3 apples, halved

Plum Sauce

Wash duck; pat dry. Stuff with halved apples. Prick skin with sharp fork several times. Roast on rack, breast side up, at 400° F. (200° C.) for the first 30 minutes; reduce to 350° F. (180° C.) for 2 hours or until tender. Baste duckling with Plum Sauce during last 30 minutes of baking.

Plum Sauce

1 medium onion
2 tablespoons (30 ml) melted butter
1 can (16 ounces or 454 g) pitted
   purple plums
1 can (6 ounces or 168 g) frozen
   lemonade

1/4 cup (50 ml) soy sauce
2 teaspoons (10 ml) mustard
1 teaspoon (5 ml) ground ginger
1 teaspoon (5 ml) Worcestershire sauce
2 drops hot pepper sauce

Assemble Blender. Put onion in pieces into blender container. Cover and blender-chop. Saute in butter. Put purple plums into blender container. Cover and process at PUREE. Add to onion. Add all remaining ingredients. Simmer, uncovered, for 15 minutes. This sauce may be made ahead and refrigerated or frozen.
Yield: 4 servings

LEMON CHICKEN

4 chicken legs (thigh and drumstick)
2 whole chicken breasts, split into
   halves
1 teaspoon (5 ml) garlic salt
2 teaspoons (10 ml) paprika

1 teaspoon (5 ml) crushed oregano
1/2 teaspoon fresh grated lemon peel
1/3 cup (75 ml) fresh lemon juice
1/2 cup (125 ml) water
Parsley, optional

Season chicken pieces well with garlic salt. Sprinkle with paprika. Place in shallow baking pan skin-side down. Assemble Blender. Place remaining ingredients in blender container; cover and blend at BEAT. Pour over chicken. Bake, uncovered at 400° F. (200° C.) about 35 minutes. Turn chicken over, and continue baking, basting with pan drippings, until done, about 20 minutes. Garnish with parsley, if desired.

Yield: 4-6 servings

VEAL AU PORTO

Port and cognac help give this veal dish its flair.

Flour
1-1/2 to 2 pounds (0.8-1 kg) veal
   scallops, sliced very thin
2 tablespoons (30 ml) olive oil
Salt and pepper
1 large onion, thin-sliced
1/4 cup (50 ml) port wine

1 cup (250 ml) heavy cream
1 teaspoon (5 ml) tarragon
1/2 teaspoon (2 ml) basil
2 egg yolks
2 tablespoons (30 ml) cognac
1 tablespoon (15 ml) lemon juice

Lightly flour veal scallops. In heavy skillet, brown scallops in olive oil. Salt and pepper lightly before turning. Turn and brown other side; season again. Remove from skillet. Assemble Salad Maker. Slice onion as indicated above. Add onion slices to pan, and cook until soft and golden. Remove and place on top of veal. Add port to the pan, and stir to remove all particles stuck to the sides and bottom. Add half the cream and cook until slightly thickened. Add tarragon and basil.

Assemble Mixer. In small mixer bowl beat egg yolks at #4 with remainder of cream. Add a little of the hot cream from skillet; stir and return all to the skillet. Add cognac and lemon juice. If a stronger flavor is desired, add more cognac. Add veal and onions, and heat until mixture bubbles and veal is completely heated. Serve immediately.

Yield: 3-4 servings

CURRIED FISH STEAKS

4 halibut, salmon or other firm fish
    steaks, about 3/4-inch (1.8 cm)
    thick
Salad oil
Salt and pepper to taste
3/4 cup (200 ml) mayonnaise or
    salad dressing

1/4 cup (50 ml) tomato catsup
2 teaspoons (10 ml) fresh grated orange
    peel
2 tablespoons (30 ml) orange juice
1/4 teaspoon (1 ml) curry powder
Parsley, optional

Brush fish steaks lightly with oil. Sprinkle with salt and pepper to taste. Broil about 5 minutes on each side. Brush with additional oil, if needed. Meanwhile, assemble Blender. Place mayonnaise or salad dressing, tomato catsup, orange peel, orange juice and curry powder in blender container. Cover and process at WHIP until well blended. Serve sauce with fish steaks. Garnish with parsley, if desired.
Yield: 4 servings (about 1-1/2 cups [375 ml] of sauce)

LAMB AND EGGPLANT CASSEROLE

Based on the Greek specialty of Moussaka, this tasty casserole is an easy dish and could well become a family favorite.

1/2 pound (227 g) Mozzarella
    cheese cubes
1 can (8 ounces or 227 g) tomato
    sauce
1 small wedge onion
1/4 cup (50 ml) grated Parmesan cheese

1 medium eggplant, quartered
1/3 cup (75 ml) butter
1 pound (454 g) ground lamb
1/2 teaspoon (2 ml) salt
Dash pepper

Preheat oven to 350° F. (180° C.). Assemble Blender. Blender-grate Mozzarella cheese; empty onto waxed paper and set aside. Put tomato sauce, onion and Parmesan cheese into blender and blender-chop onion. Set aside. Assemble Salad Maker with the Thick Slicer. Slice eggplant. Melt butter; add eggplant slices and cook over low heat until lightly browned on both sides. Place in a shallow 2-quart (2 liter) baking pan; reserve drippings. Add ground lamb, salt and pepper to drippings. Cook until lamb is lightly browned. Drain, if necessary. Place over eggplant. Add blended tomato sauce, and bake for 20 minutes. Add Mozzarella cheese. Bake 10 more minutes or until cheese is melted.
Yield: 6 servings

NUTTY FISH

1 cup (250 ml) chunk-style peanut
    butter
1/4 cup (50 ml) light brown
    sugar
1/4 cup (50 ml) soy sauce
1/4 cup (50 ml) lemon juice

1/2 teaspoon (2 ml) liquid hot pepper
    sauce
1/2 teaspoon (2 ml) nutmeg
1/4 teaspoon (1 ml) garlic powder
2 pounds (1 kg) fish fillets
1 medium onion, thin-sliced

Assemble Blender. Put peanut butter, brown sugar, soy sauce, lemon juice, hot pepper sauce, nutmeg and garlic powder into blender container. Cover and process at BLEND. Wash and dry fish fillets. Place fillets in single layer in shallow foil-lined baking pan. Spread peanut butter mixture evenly over fish. Assemble Salad Maker. Slice onion as indicated above. Arrange over fish. Bake at 350° F. (180° C.) until fish flakes easily, about 20 minutes.
Yield: 6 servings

CHICKEN DIJON

Dijon is a city most known for its mustard. Produced since the 15th century, it gives a savory flavoring to chicken.

1 3-pound (1.5 kg) chicken, cut
    into 12 pieces
Flour seasoned with salt
2 tablespoons (30 ml) olive oil
2 tablespoons (30 ml) butter
Bay leaf

2 tablespoons (30 ml) Dijon mustard
1/2 teaspoon (2 ml) cornstarch
4 tablespoons (60 ml) sour cream
1/2 teaspoon (2 ml) salt
Dash cayenne pepper
Dash curry powder

Roll chicken pieces in seasoned flour. Heat oil and butter in large heavy skillet. When sizzling, brown chicken on all sides. Reduce heat; add bay leaf. Cover skillet; cook over low heat until chicken is tender, about 15 minutes. Meanwhile, assemble Blender. Place Dijon mustard, cornstarch, sour cream, salt, cayenne pepper and curry powder in blender container. Cover and process at BEAT until smooth. Remove chicken to heated platter, and keep warm. Discard bay leaf. Remove excess fat from skillet, leaving bits of chicken on bottom of pan. Add Dijon sauce mixture; combine with pan scrapings. Place over low heat; stir until smooth and hot. Pour over chicken, and serve.
Yield: 6 servings

FRIED FISH PATTIES

1 pound (454 g) frozen haddock,
    cod or pollock fillets
1 medium onion, cut in eighths
5 medium potatoes, pared
1/4 teaspoon (1 ml) pepper

2 teaspoons (10 ml) Worcestershire sauce
1/4 teaspoon (1 ml) hot pepper sauce
4 sprigs fresh parsley
3 tablespoons (45 ml) butter

In saucepan heat 1 quart water to boiling. Drop in fish pieces and simmer 5-10 minutes until fish flakes. Remove fish and cool. Put onions and parsley in a Mini-Blend container and process 3 cycles at CHOP. Assemble Salad Maker with Shredder Disc. Shred potatoes. Flake fish and combine with the onions and shredded potatoes. Add remaining ingredients, except butter and mix well. Melt butter on grill or skillet. Form mixture into 12 patties and fry. Serve with Dill Sauce.
Yield: 6 servings

Dill Sauce

6 tablespoons (90 ml) butter
6 tablespoons (90 ml) flour
2 cups (500 ml) milk
1/8 teaspoon (1/2 ml) paprika
3/4 teaspoon (3 ml) dried dillweed

3/4 teaspoon (3 ml) salt
1/4 teaspoon (1 ml) parsley flakes
1/8 teaspoon (1/2 ml) basil
1/8 teaspoon (1/2 ml) oregano

Assemble Blender. Put butter, flour and milk into blender container, cover and process at WHIP until blended. Pour into saucepan, add seasonings and cook over low heat, stirring constantly until thick.
Yield: 2 cups sauce

FRENCH COUNTRY ONION PIE

1/4 pound (113 g) butter
3/4 cup (200 ml) all-purpose flour
1/2 cup (125 ml) small curd creamed
    cottage cheese
Salt
2 pounds (1 kg) onions, diced

1/4 pound (113 g) butter
3 eggs plus 1 yolk
3 teaspoons (15 ml) caraway seeds
Salt and pepper
3 slices bacon, fried crisp and crumbled

Assemble Mixer. Put butter, flour, cottage cheese and salt into large mixer bowl. Mix at #1 until pastry is well blended; form into a ball. Wrap in foil and chill well in refrigerator. Roll to 1/4-inch (0.6 cm) and line a 9-inch (23 cm) pie pan with pastry dough. Flute edges. Assemble Salad Maker. Dice onions using French Fry Cutter. Melt butter and saute onions in it until golden. Cool. Add eggs, caraway seeds, salt and pepper to taste. Mix and pour into pie shell. Sprinkle with crumbled bacon. Bake at 350° F. (180° C.) for 1 hour.
Yield: 6-8 servings

BROILED CHICKEN

1/4 pound (113 g) butter, softened
1 tablespoon (15 ml) lemon juice
1 tablespoon (15 ml) soy sauce
2 cloves garlic, finely minced
1/4 teaspoon (1 ml) thyme
1 teaspoon (5 ml) tarragon

1 2-1/2 to 3 pound (1.3-1.5 kg) broiling
    chicken, quartered
Pepper
1 tablespoon (15 ml) kosher salt
Chopped parsley

Assemble Mixer. Cream butter in small mixer bowl at #4, adding lemon juice a few drops at a time. Then slowly beat in soy sauce, minced garlic, thyme and tarragon. Spread this butter paste on both sides of chicken pieces with a pastry brush. Drizzle any liquid in the bowl over the chicken. Reserve a little paste for basting.

Place chicken skin side down on rack about midway in the oven. Season lightly with pepper and kosher salt. Baste chicken every 5 minutes, first with remainder of butter paste, then with drippings. Turn after 15 minutes (be careful not to pierce skin). Season again with pepper and the remainder of the kosher salt. Broil 30 minutes more, basting twice. When done, remove to a warm platter and sprinkle with chopped parsley.
Yield: 6 servings

CASSOULET

As the national French favorite, this noble bean stew comes from southwestern France. It has risen from a country casserole to one of the great specialties of French domestic cooking. It must be cooked slowly to blend all flavors and should include a good amount of white beans with meats and poultry including pork, lamb, roast duck, sausage, bacon or smoked ham. There are many variations depending on locality and ingredients on hand in the kitchen.

4 cups (1000 ml) dried pea beans, washed and drained
2 quarts (2 liters) water
1 tablespoon (15 ml) salt
2 cloves garlic, mashed
2 carrots, quartered
2 onions, studded with two cloves each
Bouquet garni (parsley, celery, bay leaf and thyme in cheesecloth bag)
1/4 cup (50 ml) diced salt pork
2 Bermuda onions, cut into 1-inch pieces

1 cup (250 ml) shallot or green onion pieces
1 cup (250 ml) celery pieces
2 tablespoons (30 ml) oil
1-1/2 pounds (.75 kg) lean boneless pork, cubed
1 pound (454 g) boneless lamb, cubed
1 cup (250 ml) tomato sauce or juice
1 cup (250 ml) dry white wine
1 garlic sausage, sliced
1 roast duck, with meat removed from bones and cut into bite-size pieces

Combine pea beans, water and salt. Let stand overnight. Add garlic, carrots, whole onions, bouquet garni and salt pork. Bring to a boil. Simmer, covered, for 1 hour. Assemble Blender and using the water-chop method, chop the onions, shallots or green onions and celery. Heat oil in large skillet. Add pork and lamb. Brown on all sides. Add to bean mixture. In the same skillet, cook chopped onions, shallots or green onions and celery until soft. Add tomato sauce and wine. Simmer 5 minutes. Add to beans with garlic sausage. Simmer, covered, for 1 hour, or until both beans and meat are tender. If necessary, add a little water to prevent burning.

Preheat oven to 350° F. (180° C.). Skim off excess fat. Discard bouquet garni. Transfer half the mixture to a large casserole and cover with duck. Add remaining mixture and top with duck. Bake, covered, at 350° F. (180° C.) for about 40 minutes. Stir a few times adding a little water, if necessary. This recipe could be divided, and half of it frozen for future use.
Yield: 12-15 servings

PORTUGUESE MEATBALLS

1 pound (454 g) stew meat
1 teaspoon (5 ml) salt
1/4 teaspoon (1 ml) pepper
2 eggs, beaten
1/4 pound (113 g) bacon, diced
1/4 cup (50 ml) chopped parsley
1 garlic clove, minced

All-purpose flour
1 medium onion
Oil
4 tomatoes
2 tablespoons (30 ml) beef bouillon
    or water

Assemble Food Grinder with Fine Disc. Grind meat, salt and pepper. Add the eggs. Cook bacon until browned; drain and add to the meat with half the parsley and minced clove garlic. Shape into walnut-size balls and roll in flour. Assemble Blender. Put onion into blender container. Cover and process at CHOP. Cook onion in the hot oil until golden. Meanwhile, peel the tomatoes and blender-chop. Add with the remaining parsley and bouillon or water to the onions. Add the meatballs, and simmer, uncovered, for about 30 minutes.
Yield: 6 servings

INDONESIAN-STYLE BEEF

Peanuts and bananas, two of Indonesia's most popular ingredients, are combined in this dish for an unusual exotic taste.

1-1/2 pounds (680 g) flank steak,
    scored on both sides
1/2 cup (125 ml) soy sauce
1/2 cup (125 ml) salted peanuts
2 tablespoons (30 ml) lemon juice
1 tablespoon (15 ml) molasses

1 clove garlic
1/2 teaspoon (2 ml) cayenne pepper
1/2 teaspoon (2 ml) ground ginger
2 large bananas
Rice

Cut flank steak lengthwise into 6 long strips. Place in a shallow dish. Assemble Blender. Place soy sauce, peanuts, lemon juice, molasses, garlic, cayenne pepper and ground ginger into blender container. Cover and blend at WHIP until smooth. Pour over flank steak. Refrigerate 2-3 hours. Cut bananas into 1-inch (2.5 cm) chunks. Thread steak strips on skewers alternately with banana chunks. Reserve leftover marinade. Broil about 5 minutes. Turn; brush with marinade, and continue broiling until done. Serve with hot rice.
Yield: 4-6 servings

CIOPPINO

Corn, one of the oldest foods in the world, is a feature of this unique stew. It is known throughout the world in many different adaptations. The recipe is Italian and a fine example of Italian home cooking.

4 ears fresh corn
3 cups (750 ml) onions, cubed
1 green pepper, cut into eighths
1/4 cup (50 ml) olive or salad oil
2-1/2 teaspoons (12 ml) minced garlic
1 can (1 pound 12 ounces or 790 g) tomatoes, broken up
1 can (8 ounces or 227 g) tomato sauce
1-1/2 cups (375 ml) dry white wine
1-1/2 teaspoons (7 ml) salt
1 teaspoon (5 ml) Italian seasoning
1/4 teaspoon (1 ml) sugar
1/4 teaspoon (1 ml) black pepper
3-1/2 pounds (1.8 kg) firm-fleshed fish fillets, cut into chunks
3/4 pound (336 g) raw shrimp, peeled and deveined
4-5 sprigs parsley, chopped
1 can (10-1/4 ounces or 280 g) whole clams or 12 fresh clams

Remove husks and silks from corn; cut into 1-inch (2.5 cm) pieces. Set aside. Assemble Blender. Blender water-chop onion and pepper. Drain well. In a Dutch oven or large saucepan heat oil. Add onion, green pepper and garlic; saute 8 minutes, stirring occasionally. Add tomatoes, tomato sauce, white wine, salt, Italian seasoning, sugar and black pepper. Bring to boiling point. Reduce heat; simmer, covered, 30 minutes. Add fish fillets. Return to boiling point. Reduce heat and simmer, covered, 15 minutes. Then add reserved corn chunks with shrimp and parsley; simmer 15-20 minutes or until fish flakes easily. Add clams and cook only until hot, or with fresh clams, cook until opened. Serve with Italian bread.
Yield: 6-8 servings

TARRAGON CHICKEN

1 3-pound (1.5 kg) chicken, cut
    into 10 pieces
1 tablespoon (15 ml) olive oil
1 tablespoon (15 ml) butter
1 teaspoon (5 ml) salt
1/4 teaspoon (1 ml) white pepper

2 sprigs fresh tarragon or 1 tablespoon
    of dried tarragon
4 egg yolks
1/2 teaspoon (2 ml) cornstarch
2 cups (500 ml) milk
4 ounces (113 g) cubed Bonbel cheese
Salt and pepper to taste

Cook chicken in combined oil and butter, browning on all sides. Add salt, pepper and tarragon. Cover and cook over low heat for 25 minutes, or until tender. Discard tarragon sprigs. Place chicken on platter and keep warm. Drain fat from pan. Put the egg yolks, cornstarch and milk into the blender container with cubed cheese. Cover blender, grate the cheese, then pour mixture into pan in which chicken was cooked, scraping the bottom with a wooden spoon to loosen bits of chicken. Cook over low heat, stirring until sauce bubbles and thickens. Season with salt and pepper to taste. Pour sauce over chicken and serve.
Yield: 5-6 servings

SALMON-ZUCCHINI QUICHE

A good, easy-to-prepare quiche. A fine last minute supper entree.

2-1/2 ounces (70 g) Parmesan cheese
1/2 pound (227 g) zucchini, washed
1 small onion, finely diced
3 eggs
1 tablespoon (15 ml) lemon juice
1/4 teaspoon (1 ml) salt

1/4 teaspoon (1 ml) dried dillweed
1/8 teaspoon (1/2 ml) pepper
4 sprigs fresh parsley
1 can (8 ounces or 227 g) red salmon,
    drained and flaked
Pie crust (unbaked)

Preheat oven to 375° F. (190° C.). Assemble Salad Maker with Shredder Disc. Shred cheese and set aside before shredding zucchini. In a small saucepan combine zucchini and onion. Add enough water to cover, bring to a boil and cook just until tender, about 3 minutes. Drain well, pressing out the liquid. Put eggs, lemon juice and seasoning into blender container. Cover and process at WHIP. Add parsley and process 2 cycles at CHOP. Combine zucchini, onion, cheese and salmon. Pour into an 8-inch unbaked pie crust. Bake 30-40 minutes or until set.
Yield: 6 servings

CHICKEN MOUSSE

3 cups (750 ml) skinned, boneless
  chicken breasts, cubed
Salt and pepper to taste
1/4 teaspoon (1 ml) nutmeg
1/4 teaspoon (1 ml) cayenne pepper

2 cups (500 ml) light cream
1 egg white, lightly beaten
Sauce Aurore
Chopped Parsley

Assemble Blender. Put a few chicken cubes into blender container. Cover and process at LIQUEFY until smooth. Scrape into a bowl. Repeat until all the chicken has been blended. Add salt, pepper, nutmeg and cayenne pepper. Chill well. Set the bowl in a container of ice cubes. Gradually beat in cream. Beat in egg white. Chill. Place in buttered 1-1/2-quart (1.5 liter) mold. Smooth top with spatula. Cover with a buttered ring of parchment paper. Place in a baking dish; add about 1-inch (2.5 cm) of boiling water. Bake at 400° F. (200° C.) for 25-35 minutes. Unmold and spoon some sauce over it for color. Sprinkle with chopped parsley. Put remaining sauce in gravyboat and pass around individually.

Sauce Aurore

4 tablespoons (60 ml) butter
3 tablespoons (45 ml) chopped onion
3 tablespoons (45 ml) chopped
  shallots
2 cups (500 ml) tomatoes, seeded
Salt and pepper
1 bay leaf

1/2 teaspoon (2 ml) tarragon
1/2 teaspoon (2 ml) thyme
1-1/2 tablespoons (23 ml) all-purpose
  flour
1 cup (250 ml) chicken broth
1/2 cup (125 ml) heavy cream

Melt one tablespoon (15 ml) butter. Assemble Blender. Put onion and shallots into blender container and blender chop. Saute in melted butter. Meanwhile, put tomatoes into blender container. Cover and process at PUREE. Add to onions and shallots. Then add salt and pepper to taste, bay leaf, tarragon and thyme. Cook, stirring frequently, about 30 minutes. Meanwhile, melt 1 tablespoon (15 ml) butter; stir in flour. Add chicken broth, and simmer, stirring occasionally, about 10 minutes. Add tomato sauce; cook 15 minutes longer. Strain. Stir in cream. Melt remaining butter. Swirl into sauce.
Yield: 1-1/2 quarts (1.5 liters) mousse and 2-1/4 cups (550 ml) sauce

SHRIMP CROQUETTES

The blender makes quick work of preparing these croquettes.

3 to 4 slices of dry bread
3 to 4 sprigs of parsley
2 tablespoons (30 ml) butter
4 tablespoons (60 ml) flour
3/4 teaspoon (3 ml) salt
Dash pepper
1 cup (250 ml) milk

16 ounces (454 g) cooked shrimp,
    finely minced
1/2 teaspoon (2 ml) lemon juice
1 egg
2 tablespoons (30 ml) water
Oil for deep-fat frying

Blender-crumb bread. Blender-chop parsley in Mini-Blend container. In a sauce-pan, melt butter, add flour, salt and pepper. Stir and cook until a roux or paste forms. Gradually stir in milk. Cook until thick. Stir in shrimp, parsley and lemon juice. Mix well and chill. Shape into 8 balls, about 1/4 cup (50 ml) each. Dip each ball into lightly beaten egg and water mixture. Roll in bread crumbs. Reshape into cones. Fry 2 or 3 at a time until golden brown at 375° F. (190° C.) about 3 minutes. Yield: 8 croquettes (4 servings)
VARIATIONS:
Use 2 cups (500 ml) cooked chicken, finely ground; or 2 7-ounce cans (225 g each) tuna; or 1 16-ounce can (454 g) salmon, drained and boned.

FRENCH COUNTRY-STYLE PORK CHOPS

4 medium carrots, julienne sliced
2 small white turnips, julienne sliced
2 celery stalks, julienne sliced
4 leeks, white part only, julienne
    sliced
4 small white onions
3-1/2 cups (875 ml) tomatoes
1/4 teaspoon (1 ml) marjoram

1 bay leaf
1/4 cup (50 ml) chopped parsley
3/4 teaspoon (4 ml) salt
1/2 teaspoon (2 ml) pepper
1/3 cup (75 ml) chicken stock
2 pounds (1 kg) blade pork chops,
    trimmed of excess fat

Assemble Salad Maker. Cut the carrots, turnips, celery and leeks with French Fry Cutter. Assemble Blender. Put onions into blender container. Cover and process at CHOP. Combine vegetables with chopped onion in large, heavy kettle, and add tomatoes, marjoram, bay leaf, chopped parsley, salt and pepper. Add chicken stock; bring to a boil. Simmer, covered, for 5 minutes. Put pork chops on top of vegetables. Cover and simmer about 1 hour, or until done. At serving time, place vegetables in center of serving dish and surround with pork chops.
Yield: 4 servings

SHRIMP REMOULADE

The name of this sauce comes from the word "remouleur" (knife grinder) because of it's cutting or piquant flavor.

2 stalks celery with leaves, cut into 1-inch pieces
3 cups (750 ml) water
Juice of 1 lemon
2 cloves garlic
1 bay leaf
1 teaspoon (5 ml) salt
8 peppercorns
4 sprigs parsley
2 pounds (2 kg) shrimp

Combine all ingredients except shrimp in a large kettle and bring to a boil. Add shrimp; cover and bring to a boil again. Uncover and cook 3 to 4 minutes for small shrimp or about 5 minutes for jumbo shrimp. Cook just until they have turned pink. Do not overcook. Drain, chill and devein the shrimp. Pour Remoulade Sauce over them.

Remoulade Sauce

1 cup (250 ml) mayonnaise
1/2 cup (125 ml) sour cream
2 green onions, cut in pieces
1 tablespoon (15 ml) lemon juice
2 teaspoons (10 ml) chopped capers
1/2 teaspoon (2 ml) tarragon
1 teaspoon (5 ml) oregano
1/2 teaspoon (2 ml) chervil
1/2 teaspoon (2 ml) garlic wine vinegar
Salt and pepper to taste

Assemble Blender. Put all ingredients into blender container. Cover and process at BLEND until mixed well. If the sauce does not taste tart enough, add a little more vinegar.
Yield: 6 servings

Chapter Seven
DESSERTS

APRICOT CUSTARD

2 cups (500 ml) milk
1/2 cup (125 ml) dried apricots
1/3 cup (75 ml) sugar

3 eggs
1/4 teaspoon (1 ml) salt

Assemble Blender. Place all ingredients into blender container. Cover and process beginning at BEAT, gradually increasing to LIQUEFY. Pour into 6 or 8 buttered custard cups. Place cups in pan of hot water. Bake at 350° F. (180° C.) about 45 minutes, or until knife inserted in center comes out clean.
Yield: 6-8 servings

FRENCH STRAWBERRY TART

Fresh strawberries and cream are featured in this elegant dessert, one of the author's favorites.

1 cup (250 ml) all-purpose flour
Dash salt
6 tablespoons (90 ml) butter, cut
    into small pieces
1 egg yolk
4 tablespoons (60 ml) confectioners'
    sugar

1 teaspoon (5 ml) vanilla extract
1/4 teaspoon (1 ml) grated lemon rind
1/2 cup (125 ml) red currant jelly
1 pint (0.5 liter) fresh strawberries
1 cup (250 ml) heavy cream
Sugar

Preheat oven to 375° F. (190° C.). Assemble Doughmaker. Sift the flour and salt into the large mixer bowl. Add the butter, egg yolk, confectioners' sugar, vanilla extract and lemon rind. Knead the ingredients until the dough is smooth. Pat out the dough onto the bottom and sides of an 8-inch (20 cm) cake pan. Prick the bottom and sides of the dough with a fork. Bake for 15-20 minutes, or until pastry is light brown. Cool.

Meanwhile, to make a glaze, put the currant jelly in a small saucepan, and melt it slowly over low heat. Cool slightly and brush with portion of the glaze over bottom of the pastry. Wash and hull strawberries, arranging them points up, over the bottom of the pastry. Brush with remaining glaze. Just before serving, assemble Mixer. In small mixer bowl whip cream at #9 until light and fluffy. Sweeten it to taste with sugar, and spoon it around the edge of the tart. Cut into wedges and serve.
Yield: 6-8 servings

CARAMEL RICE PUDDING

1 cup (250 ml) milk
1 egg
1 cup (250 ml) raisins
1/4 cup (50 ml) firmly packed dark
  brown sugar

Dash salt
1 cup (250 ml) cooked rice
Cinnamon

Assemble Blender. Put milk, egg, raisins, brown sugar and salt into blender container. Cover and process at BLEND. Pour the mixture over the rice. Spoon into 4 buttered custard cups. Sprinkle with cinnamon. Set cups in pan of hot water. Bake at 350° F. (180° C.) for 60 minutes or until knife inserted in center comes out clean.
Yield: 4 servings

STRAWBERRY BAVARIAN CREAM

The mid-to-late nineteenth century was the heyday of molded desserts, and the Bavarian reigned supreme. It was a Victorian splendor in both taste and appearance, and is still elegant, delicious, and much easier to make than it was in those days.

2 packages (16 ounces or 454 g each)
  frozen strawberries
1 tablespoon (15 ml) lemon juice
2 envelopes unflavored gelatin
1/4 cup (50 ml) cold water
1/2 cup (125 ml) sugar
1 egg

1 cup (250 ml) heavy cream
1 cup (250 ml) crushed ice, drained
2 tablespoons (30 ml) cognac,
  optional
1 package (10 ounces or 280 g) frozen
  strawberries, optional

Thaw two packages of strawberries. Drain 1/2 cup juice into saucepan and add lemon juice. Heat to boiling. Assemble Blender. Put cold water and gelatin into blender container and process at LOW or STIR to soften the gelatin. Add boiling liquid. If gelatin crystals cling to the container STOP THE BLENDER, and use a rubber spatula to push granules into the mixture. Continue to increase the speed as the ingredients increase.

When gelatin is dissolved, add cream and crushed ice while processing until the ice is liquefied. Pour contents into a 1-1/2-quart (1.5 liter) mold, which has been rinsed with cold water. Chill 20 to 30 minutes. Meanwhile, thaw a third package of strawberries to combine with cognac, if desired. Remove dessert from mold and serve with strawberry sauce.
Yield: 6 servings

PLUM WHIP

3/4 pound (340 g) fresh plums
1/4 cup (50 ml) water
1/2 teaspoon (2 ml) grated lemon rind

1/2 cup (125 ml) sugar
2 egg whites
4 slices fresh plums

Wash plums. Place in saucepan with water. Cover and cook gently for 20 minutes until tender. Assemble Blender. Put into blender container. Cover and process at PUREE. Measure 1 cup. Cool. Stir in lemon rind and half of the sugar. Meanwhile, assemble Mixer. Beat egg whites at #9 until soft peaks form. Gradually beat in remaining sugar and carefully fold into plum puree. Pile gently into sherbet glasses. Garnish with slice of fresh plum.
Yield: 4 servings

COTTAGE PUDDING

3 tablespoons (45 ml) butter,
    softened
3/4 cup (200 ml) sugar
1 egg, beaten
1-1/4 cups (300 ml) all-purpose flour

2 teaspoons (10 ml) baking powder
Dash salt
1/2 cup (125 ml) hot water
1/2 teaspoon (2 ml) vanilla extract
Pudding Sauce

Preheat oven to 350° F. (180° C.). Assemble Mixer. Cream butter and sugar in large mixer bowl at #4 until fluffy. Add beaten egg. Sift together the flour, baking powder and salt. Add to creamed mixture, and blend well. Add hot water and beat at #4 until smooth. Add vanilla extract. Pour into shallow greased 9-inch (23 cm) pan. Bake for 25 minutes. Cut into squares, and serve warm with Pudding Sauce.

Pudding Sauce

4 tablespoons (60 ml) butter,
    softened
3/4 cup (200 ml) confectioners'
    sugar, sifted

1/4 teaspoon (1 ml) vanilla extract
1 cup (250 ml) frozen strawberries
1/2 cup (125 ml) heavy cream

Assemble Mixer. Cream butter in large mixer bowl at #4; add sugar and beat until creamy. Add vanilla extract and strawberries. Set aside. In small mixer bowl, beat the heavy cream at #10 until whipped. Fold into strawberries. Do not make sauce until ready to serve.
Yield: 6-8 servings

CHESTNUT MOLD

The French call this a cake but it is actually a molded desert. We find it so rich that even a very small serving will be enough to satisfy the most avid dessert eater. It is very good and very expensive.

2 bars (4 ounces or 113 g each) sweet chocolate
1 can (15-1/2 ounces or 434 g) unsweetened whole chestnuts, drained

3/4 cup (200 ml) sugar
1/2 cup (125 ml) sweet butter, melted
Whipped cream, optional

Melt the sweet chocolate and cool. Set aside. Assemble Grinder with Fine Disc. Put chestnuts through food grinder. Stir in sugar and butter. Add chocolate and mix well. Pour into small parfait glasses and chill for several hours, or until firm. Decorate with whipped cream, if desired.
Yield: 10-12 servings

CARAMEL CUSTARD

A favorite in France and throughout South America, caramel custard's origins date back to Ancient Greece. Such long-time popularity must be deserved!

1 cup (250 ml) sugar
Dash salt
2 eggs

2 cups (500 ml) milk, scalded
1/2 teaspoon (2 ml) vanilla extract

Preheat oven to 350° F. (180° C.). In small heavy skillet heat 3/4 cup (200 ml) sugar. Stir with wooden spoon constantly until sugar melts and begins to turn brown. Pour syrup evenly into bottoms of 6 small custard cups. Let stand until syrup cools. Assemble Mixer. Add the remaining 1/4 cup (50 ml) sugar and salt to eggs in large mixer bowl and beat at #4 until ingredients are well blended. Slowly add scalded milk, stirring constantly. Add vanilla extract and stir again. Pour mixture slowly into cups over the caramel syrup, which by now should be hard.

Place cups in a pan filled with water (water should come almost to top of cups). Bake about 50 minutes or until a knife inserted in center comes out clean. Turn off oven and let cups remain 10 minutes more. Remove cups from water and chill. To serve, run knife around edge of cups and turn custard onto plates. Caramel syrup will be on top.
Yield: 6 servings

MINTED POTS DE CREME

Not too heavy or sweet, with just a hint of mint flavoring.

1 cup (250 ml) semi-sweet mint
    chocolate bits
1-1/4 cups (300 ml) light cream,
    scalded

2 egg yolks
2 tablespoons (30 ml) rum
Heavy cream
Chocolate shavings

Assemble Blender. Put mint chocolate bits, light cream, egg yolks and rum into blender container. Cover and process at BLEND until smooth. Pour into 6 pot-de-cremes or small sherbet glasses, and chill for about 3 hours. Assemble Mixer. In small mixer bowl beat amount of heavy cream desired for whipped cream. Garnish each individual serving. Top with chocolate shavings.
Yield: 6 servings

ORANGE CREME BRULEE

This classic French dessert becomes quick and easy with the food processor to help. It may be a good idea to make it a day ahead to be sure it's thoroughly chilled before putting it under the broiler. Then chill again.

2 medium oranges, peeled and cut
    into small pieces, drained
1/4 cup (50 ml) toasted slivered
    almonds
7 egg yolks
1/3 cup (75 ml) firmly packed dark
    brown sugar

Dash salt
2 cups (500 ml) heavy cream
1 teaspoon (5 ml) grated orange peel
3/4 cup (200 ml) firmly packed dark
    brown sugar

Place 2 tablespoons orange pieces and 1-1/2 teaspoons almonds in each of 10 6-ounce baking dishes. Set aside. Assemble Mixer. In small mixer bowl beat egg yolks at #4 until very thick and light. Gradually beat in dark brown sugar and salt. Scald cream in top of double boiler. Slowly stir small amount into egg yolk mixture. Add to rest of cream; stir in orange peel. Cook over boiling water, stirring constantly until mixture coats spoon. Immediately pour 1/2 cup of mixture into each baking dish. Chill. Using remaining brown sugar, place equal amount over each chilled creme in baking dish and place under broiler. Broil until sugar melts. Do not burn. Chill again until very cold. Topping will be crisp.
Yield: 10 servings

MACARONI PUDDING

Macaroni isn't everyone's idea of a dessert, but prepared this way it becomes a superb finale to any meal.

4 cups (1 liter) milk
1 cup (250 ml) elbow macaroni
3 eggs
1/2 cup (125 ml) sugar
1-1/2 teaspoons (7 ml) grated lemon peel

1 teaspoon (5 ml) vanilla extract
1 teaspoon (5 ml) nutmeg
1/2 cup (125 ml) raisins
Sour cream

Heat milk in a heavy saucepan, but do not boil. Add macaroni. Simmer, uncovered, for 8 to 10 minutes, stirring frequently. Assemble Mixer. In small mixer bowl, beat eggs at #4 until light. Add sugar and beat until thick and lemon-colored. Combine egg mixture with milk and macaroni. Add grated lemon peel, vanilla extract, nutmeg and raisins. Pour into lightly buttered 2-quart (2 liter) baking dish. Bake at 300° F. (150° C.) for 1 to 1-1/2 hours. Serve warm with a dollop of sour cream on each portion.
Yield: 6-8 servings

CHOCOLATE BREAD PUDDING

What better way to use leftover bread than to make it into a delicious dessert! This one is very unusual and tastes very good.

4 slices stale bread
1 square unsweetened chocolate,
    cut up
4 cups (1 liter) milk

2 eggs
1 cup (250 ml) sugar
1 teaspoon (5 ml) vanilla extract

Remove crusts from bread and break into small pieces. Place in saucepan with chocolate pieces and milk. Heat to scalding, stirring occasionally. Assemble Mixer. In large mixer bowl beat eggs well at #4. Add sugar and mix well. Pour hot chocolate mixture over eggs gradually, stirring constantly. Add vanilla extract and mix well. Pour into 2-quart (2 liter) baking dish, and place in pan of hot water. Bake at 350° F. (180° C.) for 1 hour, or until knife inserted in center comes out clean.
Yield: 8 servings

ROYAL PINEAPPLE MOUSSE

The pineapple has long been known as the symbol of hospitality. Here is a glamorous fresh dessert that will please everyone and is much easier to make than it looks.

1 large pineapple	1-1/2 envelopes unflavored gelatin
Juice of 1/2 lemon	1/2 cup (125 ml) cold milk
3 egg yolks	1 cup heavy cream
1/2 cup (125 ml) sugar	2 tablespoons (30 ml) Cointreau
Dash salt	Green leaves

Cut off the top of the pineapple, about 2 inches (5 cm) below the stem and save. With a sharp knife remove the edible part of the fruit. Do not break the shell. Cut away from pulp as much of the hard core as possible. Reserve pulp to use for mousse. Chill the shell with its cover since it will be used later for a container. Assemble Blender. Put pulp into blender container. Cover and process at GRATE. Make 1 cup, and add lemon juice to it. Set aside.

Assemble Mixer. Beat egg yolks, sugar and salt in large mixer bowl at #4 until thick and light. Add pineapple, and mix well. Set aside. Sprinkle gelatin on milk to soak for 5 minutes. Cook pineapple mixture in top of double boiler, stirring, until mixture coats a metal spoon. Add gelatin and stir until dissolved. Chill until mixture begins to thicken. Meanwhile, in small mixer bowl beat heavy cream at #10 until whipped. Add the Cointreau to it and fold into mixture. Fill chilled pineapple shell; chill until firm. Replace pineapple top and serve bedded on green leaves.
Yield: 6 servings

GINGER PEAR CRUMBLE

About 35 gingersnap cookies
1/4 cup (50 ml) butter, melted
1 can (1 pound 14 ounces or 840 g)
    pear halves, drained
1/4 cup (50 ml) drained syrup
1 tablespoon (15 ml) lemon juice

1/2 cup (125 ml) firmly packed dark
    brown sugar
1/4 teaspoon (1 ml) salt
1/2 teaspoon (2 ml) cinnamon
1/2 teaspoon (2 ml) ground nutmeg
Vanilla ice cream, optional

Preheat oven to 350° F. (180° C.). Assemble Blender. Blender-crumb ginger-snaps. Empty into a bowl and add melted butter. Mix and pat half the crumbs into a 1-1/2-quart (1.5 liter) baking dish. Put pears on crumbs and sprinkle with lemon juice and reserved pear syrup. Mix sugar, salt, cinnamon and nutmeg. Sprinkle on pears. Top with remaining crumbs. Bake about 25 minutes. Serve warm with vanilla ice cream, if desired.
Yield: 6 servings

APPLE BREAD PUDDING

3 slices fresh white bread
2 tablespoons (30 ml) soft butter
1 cup (250 ml) milk
4 tablespoons (60 ml) sugar
1/2 teaspoon (2 ml) cinnamon
Dash salt

2 thin strips lemon peel (2'' x 1/2'' or
    5 x 1 cm)
2 egg yolks
1-1/2 cups (375 ml) pared tart apple pieces
1/2 cup (125 ml) raisins
2 egg whites
4 tablespoons (60 ml) sugar

Heat oven to 375° F. (190° C.). Assemble Blender. Coarsely blender-crumb bread and empty into large mixer bowl. Put butter, milk, sugar, cinnamon, salt lemon peel and egg yolks into blender container, cover and process at MIX until smooth. Stop blender, add apple pieces, cover and process 1 cycle at GRATE. Pour over bread crumbs and add raisins. Assemble Mixer. Beat egg whites in small mixer bowl at #9 until soft peaks form, then add sugar gradually while continuing to beat until stiff peaks form. Fold egg whites into pudding mixture at #1 and turn into an ungreased 1-1/2-quart (1.50 liter) casserole. Bake 40-50 minutes, until a knife inserted into center comes out clean. Cool slightly before serving with vanilla sauce or cream.
Yield: 6 servings

ENGLISH TRIFLE

This old English recipe could easily be the crowning glory to any meal, but it is colorful and Christmasy-looking, and would be especially attractive as a holiday dish. It is very rich with just the hint of sherry.

1 cup (250 ml) custard
6 ladyfingers
Strawberry or raspberry jam
12 almond macaroons
18 blanched, slivered almonds
Grated rind of 1/2 lemon

1/3 cup (75 ml) sherry
1 cup (250 ml) heavy cream
2 tablespoons (30 ml) powdered sugar
Candied cherries
Pistachio nuts

Custard

2 egg yolks
2 tablespoons (30 ml) sugar

1 cup (250 ml) milk, scalded

In top of double boiler make a soft custard using egg yolks, sugar and scalded milk. Simmer, stirring constantly, until mixture thickens and coats spoon. Cool slightly. Split ladyfingers and spread with jam. Arrange in a serving dish. Cover with whole macaroons; sprinkle with almonds and grated lemon rind. Pour sherry over macaroons to soak them. Spoon custard over macaroons. Assemble Mixer. In a small mixer bowl whip heavy cream. Add powdered sugar to whipped cream, and spread over the top. Garnish with candied cherries and pistachio nuts. Refrigerate before serving.
Yield: 8 servings

Chapter Eight
BAKED GOODS

CREAMY CHEESECAKE

18 zwieback slices
1/4 cup (50 ml) butter, melted
1/2 cup (125 ml) sugar
2 packages (8 ounces or 227 g each)
    cream cheese, softened
1/4 cup (50 ml) all-purpose flour

1/4 teaspoon (1 ml) salt
4 eggs, separated
1-1/2 teaspoons (7 ml) grated lemon rind
1 tablespoon (15 ml) lemon juice
1 cup (250 ml) heavy cream

Preheat oven to 325° F. (160° C.). Assemble Salad Mixer with Shredding Disc. Process zwieback at #6. Combine with butter and 2 tablespoons of the sugar in a bowl. Press mixture firmly on bottom and sides of a 9-inch (23 cm) springform pan. Chill while making filling. Assemble Mixer. In large mixer bowl beat cream cheese; mix in 2 tablespoons of the sugar, flour and salt. Beat at #4 until light and fluffy. In small mixer bowl beat egg yolks at #4 until thick and lemon-colored; then beat into the cheese mixture. Stir in lemon rind, lemon juice and heavy cream.

In washed small mixer bowl beat egg whites at #9 until soft peaks form; beat in remaining sugar, 1 tablespoon at a time, and continue beating until mixture holds its shape. Fold into cheese mixture. Pour into prepared springform pan. Bake 1-1/2 hours or until center is firm. Turn off heat; let stand in oven 1 hour. Cool thoroughly before removing from pan.

Yield: 6-8 servings

WHIPPED CREAM CAKE

1 cup (250 ml) heavy cream
4 eggs
2 cups (500 ml) sugar
2 cups (500 ml) all-purpose flour

1 teaspoon (5 ml) baking powder
1 teaspoon (5 ml) salt
2 teaspoons (10 ml) vanilla extract
Confectioners' sugar

Preheat oven to 325° F. (160° C.). Assemble Mixer. In small mixer bowl, whip heavy cream at #9 until it stands in peaks. Set aside. In large mixer bowl cream eggs and sugar at #4 until light and fluffy. Sift dry ingredients into sugar mixture and mix together at #5 until well blended. Fold whipped cream and vanilla extract into mixture at #1. Bake for 35-45 minutes in well-greased 13 x 9-inch (33 x 23 cm) pan. Cool pan before cutting into squares. Sprinkle with confectioners' sugar.
Yield: 12-15 servings

FRENCH CHOCOLATE ROLL

1/2 cup (125 ml) sugar
6 eggs, separated
6 ounces (168 g) dark sweet chocolate
3 tablespoons (45 ml) cold strong coffee

1-1/3 cups (325 ml) heavy cream
3 tablespoons (45 ml) sugar
1 teaspoon (5 ml) vanilla extract
Confectioners' sugar

Preheat oven to 350° F. (180° C.). Assemble Mixer. In large mixer bowl beat at #4 1/2 cup sugar with egg yolks. Beat until mixture is light and creamy. Break chocolate into pieces and dissolve with cold coffee over low heat. Cool the chocolate a little and blend into egg yolk mixture. In small mixer bowl beat egg whites at #9 until stiff and fold into chocolate mixture. Line a jelly-roll pan with waxed paper. Grease paper. Spread batter over the waxed paper evenly and bake 15 minutes. Remove from oven, loosen sides and turn out onto a towel. Remove waxed paper. Roll cake and towel. Chill thoroughly.

Remove towel. Whip cream at #5, starting lower and gradually increasing the speed, and add 3 tablespoons sugar and vanilla extract. Unroll cake. Spread whipped cream on cake and roll jelly-roll fashion. Before serving, dust with confectioners' sugar.
Yield: 8 servings

RAISIN COFFEE CAKE

1/2 cup (125 ml) butter or margarine,
    softened
3/4 cup (200 ml) sugar
1 teaspoon (5 ml) vanilla extract
3 eggs
1-1/2 cups (375 ml) raisins

2 cups (500 ml) all-purpose flour
1 teaspoon (5 ml) baking powder
1 teaspoon (5 ml) baking soda
1 cup (250 ml) sour cream
Coffee Cake Topping

Preheat oven to 350° F. (180° C.). Grease and flour 1 10-inch (25 cm) tube pan. Assemble Mixer. In large mixer bowl beat butter, sugar and vanilla extract until fluffy. Blend in eggs, one at a time, and then add raisins. Sift flour with baking powder, baking soda and salt. Add alternately with sour cream. Mix until smooth. Spread half of batter in prepared tube pan. Sprinkle with half of the coffee cake topping. Bake 50 minutes, or until done. Cool 10 minutes; then turn out onto wire rack.

Coffee Cake Topping

1 cup (250 ml) pecans
1 cup (250 ml) brown sugar, firmly
    packed

2 teaspoons (10 ml) cinnamon
1/3 cup (75 ml) butter or margarine,
    softened

Assemble Blender. Blender-chop pecans coarsely. Mix brown sugar and cinnamon together in small mixer bowl. Cut in butter until crumbly. Add pecans.
Yield: 1 cake

BROWN SUGAR CAKE

1 cup (250 ml) shortening
1/2 cup (125 ml) butter, softened
2 cups (500 ml) light brown sugar
1/2 cup (125 ml) sugar
5 eggs, separated and yolks beaten

3 cups (750 ml) all-purpose flour
1/2 teaspoon (2 ml) baking powder
1 cup (250 ml) milk
1 cup (250 ml) chopped nuts
1 teaspoon (5 ml) vanilla extract

Preheat oven at 325° F. (160° C.). Assemble Mixer. In large mixer bowl cream shortening and butter at #4 until light. Add brown sugar and sugar, beating well. Stir in beaten egg yolks. Sift flour and baking powder together. Add flour mixture alternately with milk to creamed mixture. Add nuts and vanilla extract. In small mixer bowl, beat egg whites at #9 until stiff. Fold into mixture. Pour into greased and lightly floured 10-inch (25 cm) tube pan with removable bottom. Bake for 1 hour 20 minutes, or until cake tester comes out clean. Cool slightly and remove bottom from pan. Finish cooling before slicing.
Yield: 1 10-inch (25 cm) cake, 9-12 servings

MOLASSES SPONGE CAKE

1 cup (250 ml) molasses
1/2 cup (125 ml) sugar
1 egg
1/2 cup (125 ml) shortening
2-1/2 cups (625 ml) sifted all-purpose
    flour
1 teaspoon (5 ml) baking soda

1 teaspoon (5 ml) cinnamon
1/2 teaspoon (2 ml) ground ginger
1/4 teaspoon (1 ml) nutmeg
1/4 teaspoon (1 ml) ground cloves
1/2 teaspoon (2 ml) salt
1 cup (250 ml) boiling water

Preheat oven to 350° F. (180° C.). Grease a 9 x 12-inch (23 x 31 cm) pan. Assemble Mixer. In large mixer bowl, beat molasses, sugar, egg and shortening at #4 until thick and creamy. Sift all dry ingredients together three times. Add to creamed mixture, and mix until smooth. Add boiling water, and beat until smooth. Pour into well-greased pan. Bake for 35 minutes.
Yield: 9-12 servings

MADELEINES

Best publicized by the French writer Proust, who remembered this little scallop-shaped cake from his childhood, it has become a well-known French favorite.

1-1/2 cups (375 ml) butter or margarine
3 eggs
1 cup (250 ml) sugar
1 teaspoon (5 ml) grated lemon rind

1 teaspoon (5 ml) vanilla extract
1-1/2 cups (375 ml) sifted cake flour
Confectioners' sugar

Clarify butter or margarine by melting over low heat in a small saucepan; remove from heat. Pour into a 2-cup (500 ml) measure; let stand until solids settle to bottom. Measure 3/4 cup (200 ml) of the clear liquid into a 1-cup (250 ml) measure. Brush the madeleine molds with the remaining clarified butter; dust with flour, and shake out any excess. Beat eggs with sugar and lemon rind in the top of a double boiler; place over simmering water.

Assemble Mixer. Place mixture in large mixer bowl and beat at #9 for 5 minutes until thick and light. Remove from heat. Stir in vanilla extract. Fold cake flour into egg mixture; then fold in the 3/4 cup clarified butter. Spoon into prepared molds, filling each about half full. Cover any remaining batter, and let stand at room temperature. Bake at 350° F. (180° C.) for 20 minutes. Cool 5 minutes in molds on wire racks. Loosen around edges with top of a small knife; turn out onto racks, tapping gently, if necessary, to loosen from bottom. Cool completely. Dust lightly with confectioners' sugar. Repeat with rest of batter.
Yield: 4 dozen

GREEK SYRUP CAKE

2 cups (500 ml) water
2-1/2 cups (625 ml) sugar
2 teaspoons (10 ml) vanilla extract
1/2 teaspoon (2 ml) lemon juice
1/4 cup (50 ml) butter, softened

4 eggs
1 cup (250 ml) all-purpose flour
1 teaspoon (5 ml) baking powder
1 teaspoon (5 ml) salt
1 cup (250 ml) chopped walnuts

Combine water, 1-1/2 cups sugar, 1 teaspoon vanilla extract and lemon juice. Boil for 10 minutes. Cool syrup. Meanwhile, assemble Mixer. Cream butter and remaining sugar in large mixer bowl at #4 until light. Add eggs, one at a time, beating after each addition. Beat in flour, baking powder and salt. Add remaining vanilla extract and walnuts. Turn into an 8-inch (20 cm) square greased pan. Bake for 30 minutes at 350° F. (180° C.). Pour syrup over cake immediately.
Yield: 6-8 servings

FRENCH PLUM CAKE

1/2 cup (125 ml) butter or margarine,
   softened
1 cup (250 ml) sugar
1-1/2 cups (375 ml) sifted all-purpose
   flour
1/4 teaspoon (1 ml) salt
1/2 teaspoon (2 ml) cinnamon

1/4 teaspoon (1 ml) baking powder
1 can (28 ounces or 784 g) purple plums,
   drained and pitted
1 cup (250 ml) sour cream
1 egg, beaten
1 tablespoon (15 ml) sugar

Assemble Mixer. In large mixer bowl blend butter and sugar at #4. Sift flour with salt, cinnamon and baking powder. Combine with the butter mixture until all is crumbly. Reserve a half cup of this, pressing the remainder into the bottom of a 9 x 9-inch (23 x 23 cm) cake pan. Cut up drained plums, and spread evenly over the crust. Sprinkle with the reserved crust mixture. Bake at 400° F. (200° C.) for 15 minutes. Meanwhile, in small mixer bowl beat sour cream with the beaten egg and the 1 tablespoon of sugar. Remove the cake from the oven and spread the sour cream mixture over the top of the cake; continue baking in a 350° F. (180° C.) oven for about 25 minutes, or until cake is golden brown, and the topping is set. Remove from oven; cut into squares and serve warm.
Yield: 8 servings

CHOCOLATE VELVET CAKE

1 package (6 ounces or 168 g) semi-
    sweet chocolate bits
1/4 cup (50 ml) water
2-1/4 cups (550 ml) sifted, all-
    purpose flour
1 teaspoon (5 ml) baking soda
3/4 teaspoon (4 ml) salt

1-3/4 cups (450 ml) sugar
3/4 cup (200 ml) butter, softened
1 teaspoon (5 ml) vanilla extract
3 eggs
1 cup (250 ml) water
Chocolate Velvet Frosting

Combine chocolate bits and water in saucepan; stir over low heat until melted and smooth. Remove from heat. Sift flour, baking soda and salt together; set aside. Assemble Mixer. Combine sugar, butter and vanilla extract in large mixer bowl and beat at #4 until well blended. Add eggs, one at a time, beating well after each addition. Blend in melted chocolate mixture. Stir in flour mixture alternately with water. Pour into 2 greased and floured 9-inch (23 cm) cake pans. Bake at 375° F. (190° C.) for 30-35 minutes. Cool. Frost with Chocolate Velvet Frosting.

Chocolate Velvet Frosting

1 package (6 ounces or 168 g) semi-
    sweet chocolate bits
3 tablespoons (45 ml) butter
1/4 cup (50 ml) milk

1 teaspoon (5 ml) vanilla extract
1/4 teaspoon (1 ml) salt
3 cups (750 ml) sifted confectioners'
    sugar

Melt chocolate bits and butter over hot, not boiling water. Remove from heat. Assemble Mixer. Pour into large mixer bowl. Add milk, vanilla extract and salt. Mix at #4 until well blended. Beat in confectioners' sugar gradually.
Yield: 8 servings

QUICK APPLE CAKE

4 cups (1000 ml) apples, cut into
    1-inch (2.5 cm) pieces
1 cup (250 ml) chopped walnuts
1-1/2 cups (375 ml) salad oil
2 cups (500 ml) sugar
2 eggs

2 teaspoons (10 ml) vanilla extract
3 cups (750 ml) all-purpose flour
1 teaspoon (5 ml) salt
1 teaspoon (5 ml) baking soda
1/2 teaspoon (2 ml) cinnamon

Assemble Blender. Put apple pieces 1 cup at a time into blender container. Cover and process at STIR until chopped. Blender-chop walnuts. Set aside. Assemble Mixer. In large mixer bowl combine salad oil and sugar. Beat at #4; then add eggs and vanilla extract. Sift flour, baking soda and cinnamon together. Add to egg mixture, beating well. Stir in apples and walnuts. Place batter in greased 10-inch (25 cm) tube pan. Bake at 350° F. (180° C.) for 1-1/2 hours. Serve warm with whipped cream and a sprinkling of cinnamon.
Yield: 9-12 servings

OLD-FASHIONED SAND CAKE

A delicate version of the everyday pound cake. Serve plain or with ice cream.

1 pound (454 g) confectioners' sugar
1/4 teaspoon (1 ml) salt
1/4 teaspoon (1 ml) mace
1-1/2 cups (375 ml) butter
1 teaspoon (5 ml) vanilla extract

1/2 teaspoon (2 ml) almond extract
6 eggs
3-1/2 cups (875 ml) sifted all-purpose
    flour
2/3 cup (175 ml) milk

Assemble Mixer. Blend confectioners' sugar, salt and mace in large mixer bowl. Cream sugar mixture and butter at #4 until light and fluffy. Add vanilla and almond extracts. Beat eggs into mixture, one at a time, beating well after each addition. Add parts of flour and milk to creamed mixture alternately, blending well after each addition. When smooth, turn batter into greased and floured 10-inch (25 cm) tube pan. Bake at 350° F. (180° C.) 1 hour and 15 minutes, or until cake tester comes out clean, and cake is golden brown. Cool in pan 5 minutes; turn out onto cooling rack. Cool thoroughly.
Yield: 9-12 servings

SNOWCAPS

Beautiful little swirls of meringue gave this cookie its name. They are delicious and very nice served with fresh berries.

1 cup (250 ml) butter, softened
1 cup (250 ml) sugar
1 teaspoon (5 ml) almond extract
2 egg yolks
1/2 teaspoon (1 ml) salt

2-1/4 cups (550 ml) all-purpose flour
1/2 cup (125 ml) almonds
2 egg whites
1/2 cup (125 ml) firmly packed light
   brown sugar

Preheat oven to 325° F. (160° C.). Assemble Mixer. In a large mixer bowl cream butter at #4; gradually add sugar and beat until light and fluffy. Add almond extract, egg yolks, salt and continue beating until mixed. Reduce speed to #2. Add flour, gradually increasing speed if necessary, beating just until flour is blended in. Shape into 1/2 inch (1.3 cm) balls, and place about 1 inch apart on ungreased cookie sheets.

For topping, Assemble Blender. Put almonds into Mini-Blend container and process at MIX for 4 cycles. Set aside. Assemble Mixer. In a small mixer bowl beat egg whites at #9 until foamy. Gradually add light brown sugar, beating until stiff peaks form. Using 2 teaspoons, arrange about 1 teaspoon of meringue on top of each ball of dough, swirling top with top of spoon, and sprinkle with chopped almonds. Bake 18 to 20 minutes. Let stand a few minutes before removing to wire racks to cool. Store in a partially covered container.
Yield: 6-8 dozen

ALMOND ANGELS

You'll be considered an angel for making this heavenly cookie.

4 egg whites
1/4 teaspoon (1 ml) cream of tartar
1/4 teaspoon (1 ml) salt
1-1/2 cups (375 ml) sugar

1/2 teaspoon (2 ml) vanilla extract
1/2 teaspoon (2 ml) almond extract
1 cup (250 ml) blanched slivered almonds

Assemble Mixer. In large mixer bowl, whip egg whites, cream of tartar and salt at #9 until mixture holds soft peaks. Gradually beat in sugar, vanilla and almond extracts. Fold in slivered almonds. Grease cookie sheet well. Line with plain brown paper, and grease paper well. Drop mixture by teaspoonfuls onto greased paper. Bake at 250° F. (110° C.) for 50 minutes. Remove at once to wire rack to cool.
Yield: 3 dozen

RAISIN NUT DROPS

Coffee is the subtle flavoring that, mixed with raisins and nuts, yields nuggets of goodness.

1/2 cup (125 ml) vegetable shortening
1 cup (250 ml) firmly packed dark
    brown sugar
1 egg
2 cups (500 ml) sifted all-purpose
    flour
1/2 teaspoon (2 ml) baking soda

1/2 teaspoon (2 ml) salt
1 teaspoon (5 ml) ground cinnamon
1/2 teaspoon (2 ml) ground nutmeg
1/3 cup (75 ml) cold coffee
1 cup (250 ml) coarsely chopped walnuts
1 cup (250 ml) raisins

Preheat oven to 400° F. (200° C.). Assemble Mixer. In large mixer bowl beat shortening, sugar and egg at #4 until light and fluffy. Sift flour, baking soda, salt, cinnamon and nutmeg together, and add to the egg mixture, about 1/3 at a time alternating with the coffee (starting and ending with the flour mixture). Assemble Blender. Blender-chop walnuts. Fold into mixture with raisins. Chill for about an hour. Drop by teaspoonfuls, about 2 inches (5 cm) apart, onto greased cookie sheets. Bake for 8 minutes or until firm. Remove to wire racks to cool.
Yield: 4 dozen

MINCEMEAT SQUARES

Not just for Christmas—these cookies are good all year round.

1 cup (250 ml) sifted all-purpose flour
1/2 teaspoon (2 ml) cinnamon
1/2 teaspoon (2 ml) nutmeg
1/2 teaspoon (2 ml) salt
1/4 teaspoon (1 ml) baking soda
1/2 cup (125 ml) butter or margarine,
   softened

1/4 cup (50 ml) honey
1 teaspoon (5 ml) grated lemon peel
1/4 cup (50 ml) milk
1-1/2 cups (375 ml) quick or old-fashioned
   rolled oats
1 cup (250 ml) mincemeat
1 tablespoon (15 ml) fresh lemon juice

Preheat oven to 350° F. (180° C.). Sift together flour, cinnamon, nutmeg, salt and baking soda. Set aside. Assemble Mixer. In large mixer bowl cream butter until soft. Continue creaming while adding honey in a fine stream. Blend in lemon peel, milk and flour mixture. Add rolled oats, beating until thoroughly combined. Pat half of oat mixture into bottom of well-greased 8 x 8 x 2-inch (20 x 20 x 5 cm) pan. Mix together the mincemeat and lemon juice; spoon evenly over bottom layer. Drop teaspoonfuls of remaining oat mixture evenly over filling. Gently pat mixture into even layer to cover filling. Bake 25-30 minutes until light brown. Cool on wire rack. Cut into squares.

Yield: 16 squares

MEXICAN TEA COOKIES

Card players take note! These are especially tasty with a cup of chocolate about three o'clock in the afternoon, just as they are popular in Mexico.

1-1/2 cups (375 ml) blanched whole almonds
1 cup (250 ml) butter or margarine, softened
1/4 cup (50 ml) sugar

1 teaspoon (5 ml) grated orange rind
1 teaspoon (5 ml) vanilla extract
1/4 teaspoon (1 ml) salt
2 cups (500 ml) sifted all-purpose flour
Confectioners' sugar

Assemble Blender. Blender-chop almonds fine. Set aside. Assemble Mixer. Cream butter and sugar in large mixer bowl at #4. Mix in orange rind, vanilla extract and salt. Stir in almonds and flour. Chill dough if too soft for easy handling. Roll dough into small balls. Place on greased cookie sheet, and flatten each cookie slightly with the bottom of a glass. Bake at 325° F. (160° C.) for 25 minutes. While hot, roll in confectioners' sugar. Store in airtight container.
Yield: 4 dozen

ORANGE COOKIES

Orange juice and shredded coconut combine to make this simple-to-make, delicately flavored cookie.

2-1/2 cups (625 ml) sifted cake flour
1/2 teaspoon (2 ml) salt
1-1/2 teaspoons (7 ml) baking powder
1 teaspoon (5 ml) nutmeg
2/3 cup (175 ml) butter or margarine, softened

1 cup (250 ml) sugar
2 eggs, unbeaten
2 tablespoons (30 ml) grated orange rind
1/4 cup (50 ml) orange juice
3/4 cup (200 ml) shredded or flaked coconut

Preheat oven to 350° F. (180° C.). Sift together cake flour, salt, baking powder and nutmeg. Assemble Mixer. In large mixer bowl cream butter and sugar together at #4 until light and fluffy. Add eggs and grated orange rind; mix well. Add flour mixture alternately with the orange juice, beginning and ending with the flour mixture. Mix in coconut. Drop by teaspoonfuls about 2 inches (5 cm) apart onto lightly greased cookie sheets. Bake about 12 minutes until light brown.
Yield: 4 dozen

ALMOND PRETZELS

Did you know that the name, pretzel, derives from the Middle Latin, bracciatello, meaning little arms? This is a very good recipe.

1 (5 ounce or 140 g) can blanched
 almonds
1 cup (250 ml) butter or margarine,
 softened
1/2 cup (125 ml) sugar

2 egg yolks
1 teaspoon (5 ml) almond extract
2 cups (500 ml) sifted all-purpose flour
1 egg white
Colored sugar

Assemble Blender. Put almonds into blender container; cover and process at GRIND until fine and dry. Set aside. Assemble Mixer. In large mixer bowl cream butter at #4 until smooth. Beat in sugar, egg yolks, one at a time, and almond extract. Beat until mixture is light and fluffy. Add flour, then almonds, alternately, until evenly blended. Divide dough in half. On waxed paper, shape each half into a 12-inch (31 cm) roll; refrigerate 20 minutes.

Preheat oven to 350° F. (180° C.). Butter 1 or 2 cookie sheets. Cut off 1/2 inch (1 cm) of dough at a time and roll with fingers into a 5-inch (8 cm) long strip. Place on cookie sheets and loop ends to make pretzel shape. Bake 15-20 minutes or until golden. Remove to wire racks to cool. Keep in a cool place. To decorate, assemble Blender. In small mixer bowl beat egg white until foamy. With pastry brush, brush pretzels with egg white, then coat with colored sugar crystals.
Yield: 4 dozen

VIENNESE WALNUT COOKIES

1-1/3 cups (325 ml) walnuts
1/2 cup (125 ml) butter, softened
1/3 cup (75 ml) sugar

1/4 teaspoon (1 ml) salt
1 teaspoon (5 ml) vanilla extract
1-1/4 cups (300 ml) sifted all-purpose flour

Assemble Blender. Blender-chop walnuts. Set aside. Assemble Mixer. Cream butter, sugar, salt and vanilla extract in large mixer bowl at #4 until light. Remove beaters from mixer arm and place dough hooks in the dough hook sockets. Blend in flour and walnuts. Knead at #10 until thoroughly combined. Chill 30 minutes. Roll on a lightly-floured board to a little less than 1/4-inch (0.6 cm) thickness. Cut with 2-inch (5 cm) cookie cutter. Bake on ungreased cookie sheets at 350° F. (180° C.) for 15 minutes, until lightly browned. Cool on wire racks.
Yield: 4 dozen

GINGERSNAPS

The pungent aroma of ginger helps to make this old-fashioned cookie one of America's long-time favorites.

3/4 cup (200 ml) butter or margarine,
    softened
3/4 cup (200 ml) vegetable oil
2 cups (500 ml) sugar
2 eggs
1/2 cup (125 ml) molasses

4 cups (1000 ml) all-purpose flour
2 teaspoons (10 ml) baking soda
2 teaspoons (10 ml) cinnamon
2 teaspoons (10 ml) ground cloves
2 teaspoons (10 ml) ginger

Assemble Mixer. Cream butter with oil and sugar in large mixer bowl at #4 until fluffy. Add eggs and molasses; beat until blended. Sift together flour, baking soda, cinnamon, cloves and ginger. Add gradually to creamed mixture, beating well. Adjust mixer speed as mixture becomes heavier. Mix well; then cover and chill several hours or overnight. Dough will be soft. Roll out thin on floured pastry board, and cut with cookie cutters. Bake on ungreased cookie sheets for 5 minutes at 400° F. (200° C.). Remove to wire racks to cool.
Yield: 11 dozen

ALMOND BUTTER COOKIES

Frosted with a sweet and colorful frosting, these cookies are a rich favorite.

1 cup (250 ml) butter, softened
3 tablespoons (45 ml) sugar
1 teaspoon (5 ml) almond extract
2 cups (500 ml) all-purpose flour

1/2 teaspoon (2 ml) salt
Unblanched sliced almonds
Frosting

Preheat oven to 400° F. (200° C.). Assemble Mixer. In large mixer bowl cream butter at #4. Gradually add sugar and almond extract. Continue beating until blended. Sift together flour and salt. Gradually add to the creamed mixture, adjusting speed as needed. Chill mixture for ease in handling. Shape into balls, about 3/4-inch (1.5 cm) in diameter. Place on ungreased cookie sheets. With bottom of glass dipped in flour, flatten to 1/4-inch (0.6 cm) thickness. Bake 5-6 minutes. Remove to wire rack to cool. Place about 1/2 teaspoon (2 ml) frosting on each cookie. Top with almond slice.

Frosting

1 cup (250 ml) confectioners' sugar
4 tablespoons (60 ml) butter, softened

2 tablespoons (30 ml) cream
1/2 teaspoon (2 ml) vanilla extract

Assemble Mixer. Place all ingredients in small mixer bowl. Beat until smooth and creamy at #4.
Yield: 3-1/2 dozen

BRAN PECAN SQUARES

1 cup (250 ml) pecans
1 cup (250 ml) butter or margarine,
    softened
2 cups (500 ml) firmly-packed light
    brown sugar

1 egg
1 cup (250 ml) whole-bran cereal
3 cups (750 ml) all-purpose flour
2 teaspoons (10 ml) baking powder

Preheat oven to 350° F. (180° C.). Assemble Blender. Blender-chop pecans. Set aside. Assemble Mixer. In large mixer bowl cream butter; then gradually add sugar and egg and beat at #4 until light and fluffy. Stir in bran cereal and chopped pecans. Remove beaters from mixer arm and place dough hooks in dough hook sockets. Mix flour with baking powder and add gradually to mixture. Knead at #10 until ingredients are well combined. Press dough into greased 10 x 15-inch (25 x 37 cm) pan. Bake for 30 minutes. Remove from oven and cut into squares. Cool and remove from pan.
Yield: 20 squares

SESAME COOKIES

The nutlike sesame seeds were brought to the American South by the African slaves. They make a wonderfully crunchy topping.

1/2 cup (125 ml) butter or margarine,
    softened
6 tablespoons (90 ml) sugar
2 tablespoons (30 ml) dark brown
    sugar
1 egg

1 teaspoon (5 ml) vanilla extract
1-1/2 cups (375 ml) all-purpose flour
3/4 teaspoon (4 ml) baking powder
1/4 teaspoon (1 ml) salt
Sesame seeds

Preheat oven to 350° F. (180° C.). Assemble Mixer. In large mixer bowl cream butter, sugar and brown sugar at #4 until light and fluffy. Add egg and vanilla extract, and continue to mix. Add flour, baking powder and salt to creamed mixture. Mix well. Roll in balls the size of small walnuts and dip tops into sesame seeds, flattening cookies slightly. Put 2 inches (5 cm) apart on ungreased cookie sheets. Bake for 15-20 minutes. Check for doneness; bottoms should be golden brown. Remove to wire racks to cool.
Yield: 3 dozen

WHEAT THINS

Packed in a French canning jar tied with a ribbon, these multi-shaped cookies are a great gift idea.

1 cup (250 ml) butter, softened
2/3 cup (175 ml) sugar
2 cups (500 ml) sifted all-purpose
    flour
1 teaspoon (5 ml) baking powder

1/2 teaspoon (2 ml) salt
1 cup (250 ml) whole wheat flour
1/2 teaspoon (2 ml) anise seed*
5-6 tablespoons (75-90 ml) water
Sugar

Preheat oven to 350° F. (180° C.). Assemble Mixer. In large mixer bowl cream butter and sugar at #4 until fluffy. Sift together flour, baking powder, salt, whole wheat flour and anise seed. Remove beaters from mixer arm and place dough hooks in dough hook sockets. Add the sifted dry ingredients to the creamed mixture. Sprinkle 5 to 6 tablespoons water over mixture so that dough will be moist and hold together. Knead at #10 until thoroughly combined. Roll out half at a time on floured surface to 1/8-inch (0.3 cm) thickness. Cut into geometric shapes with cookie cutters. Sprinkle with sugar. Place on greased cookie sheets and bake for about 15 minutes.
Yield: 5-1/2 dozen

* If you like anise flavor, you may add a little more.

BUTTERNUT BARS

3/4 cup (200 ml) butter, softened
3/4 cup (200 ml) sugar
1 egg yolk
1 teaspoon (5 ml) vanilla extract

1-3/4 cups (450 ml) all-purpose flour
1/2 teaspoon (2 ml) salt
1 egg white
3/4 cup (200 ml) blender-chopped nuts

Preheat oven to 325° F. (160° C.). Assemble Mixer. Cream butter and sugar in large mixer bowl at #4 until light and fluffy. Beat in egg yolk and vanilla extract. Stir flour and salt together. Add gradually to creamed mixture at #10. Mix until well blended. Pat dough evenly into an ungreased 13 x 9 x 2-inch (33 x 23 x 5 cm) pan. Brush top lightly with egg white, sprinkle with nuts. Bake 30 minutes. Cool slightly in pan. Cut into bars; cool completely before removing bars from pan.
Yield: 3 dozen

CHOCOLATE CHIP DATE COOKIES

An interesting variation to a familiar recipe.

2 cups (500 ml) chopped dates
2-1/4 cups (550 ml) all-purpose flour
1 teaspoon (5 ml) baking soda
1 teaspoon (5 ml) salt
1 cup (250 ml) butter, softened
3/4 cup (200 ml) sugar

3/4 cup (200 ml) firmly-packed dark
    brown sugar
1 teaspoon (5 ml) vanilla extract
2 eggs
2 cups (500 ml) semi-sweet chocolate
    bits

Preheat oven to 375° F. (190° C.). Toss dates in part of the 2-1/4 cups of flour. Assemble Blender and chop 1 cup at a time. Combine flour (do not sift), baking soda, salt and chopped dates; set aside. Assemble Mixer. Place butter, sugar, brown sugar and vanilla extract in large mixer bowl. Beat at #4 until smooth. Beat in eggs. Gradually add flour mixture; mix well. Stir in chocolate bits. Drop from a teaspoon onto ungreased cookie sheets. Bake 8-10 minutes.
Yield: Approximately 8 dozen

PISTACHIO LEAVES

These cookies look pretty displayed on a white plate.

3/4 cup (200 ml) butter, softened
1 cup (250 ml) sugar
2 eggs
1 teaspoon (5 ml) lemon extract
2-1/4 cups (550 ml) all-purpose flour
1-1/2 teaspoons (7 ml) baking powder
1/2 teaspoon (2 ml) salt

2 egg yolks
2 teaspoons (10 ml) water
1/3 cup (75 ml) sugar
1/4 cup (50 ml) finely chopped pistachio
    nuts
1-1/2 teaspoons (7 ml) grated lemon peel

Preheat oven to 350° F. (180° C.). Assemble Mixer. In large mixing bowl cream butter at #4. Gradually add sugar and beat until light and fluffy. Beat in eggs and lemon extract. Combine flour, baking powder and salt. Reduce speed to #2 and gradually add flour mixture just until blended. Chill for ease in handling. Blend egg yolks with water and set aside. Assemble Blender. Combine sugar, nuts and lemon peel in "Mini-Blend" container and dry chop. Set aside. Take one-fourth of the dough at a time. Roll on floured surface to 1/8-inch (0.3 cm) thickness. Cut with a leaf-shaped cookie cutter. Brush each cookie with egg mixture, and sprinkle with nut mixture. Place on ungreased cookie sheet. Bake for 8 minutes.
Yield: 11 dozen

COCONUT CHEWS

Coconut is the fruit of a palm, native to Malaya. It is a welcome ingredient in these tasty cookies.

1/4 cup (50 ml) butter or margarine,
    softened
1 cup (250 ml) sugar
1 egg
1 tablespoon (15 ml) grated lemon peel

2 tablespoons (30 ml) lemon juice
1 cup (250 ml) flaked coconut
1 cup (250 ml) sifted all-purpose flour
1 teaspoon (5 ml) baking powder
1/2 teaspoon (2 ml) salt

Preheat oven to 350° F. (180° C.). Assemble Mixer. In large mixer bowl cream butter at #4; add sugar gradually, beating until fluffy. Add egg, grated lemon peel and lemon juice. Beat until smooth. Stir in coconut. Sift together dry ingredients, and add all at once to cream mixture. Mix well at #5. The batter should be crumbly. Spread batter into greased 8 x 8 x 2-inch (20 x 20 x 5 cm) cake pan. Bake for 30-35 minutes. Let stand in pan a few minutes before cutting into bars and removing from pan. Cool on wire rack.
Yield: 20 bars

LINZER BARS

Adapted from Austria's famous Linzertorte, these bars go back to a tradition of Vienna, at one time the undisputed capital of the confectioner's art.

1-1/2 cups (375 ml) walnuts
3/4 cup (200 ml) butter, softened
1/2 cup (125 ml) sugar
1 egg
1/2 teaspoon (2 ml) grated lemon peel

1/4 teaspoon (1 ml) salt
1/2 teaspoon (2 ml) cinnamon
1/4 teaspoon (1 ml) ground cloves
2 cups (500 ml) sifted all-purpose flour
1 cup (250 ml) raspberry jam

Preheat oven to 325 F. (160° C.). Assemble Blender. Blender-grate walnuts. Set aside. Assemble Mixer. Cream butter with sugar, egg, lemon peel, salt, cinnamon and ground cloves in large mixer bowl at #4. Blend in flour and walnuts. Set aside about a quarter of the dough for lattice top. Pat remaining dough into bottom and about 1/2-inch (1 cm) up sides of a greased 9-inch (23 cm) square pan. Spread with raspberry jam. Make pencil-shaped strips of remaining dough by rolling it against floured board with palms of hands. Arrange in lattice pattern over top, pressing ends against dough on sides of pan. Bake about 45 minutes, until lightly browned. Cool in pan; then cut into bars.
Yield: 2 dozen

FRUIT BARS

Nuts, fruits and raisins make this a rich and flavorful cookie.

1 cup (250 ml) nuts
1 cup (250 ml) golden raisins
2 cups (500 ml) seedless raisins
1 cup (250 ml) candied fruit bits
1 cup (250 ml) dates, cut in large
    pieces and coated with 1/4 cup
    (50 ml) all-purpose flour

4 eggs
1 cup (250 ml) firmly packed brown sugar
1-1/2 teaspoons (7 ml) salt
1 tablespoon (15 ml) grated orange rind
1 teaspoon (5 ml) vanilla extract
3/4 cup (200 ml) all-purpose flour
Orange Glaze

Preheat oven to 325° F. (160° C.). Assemble Blender. Blender-chop nuts. Combine with raisins, candied fruit bits and dates coated with flour. Set aside. Assemble Mixer. In large mixer bowl beat eggs at #9 until foamy. Add brown sugar, salt, orange rind and vanilla extract. Beat just until blended. Reduce speed to #4. Stir in flour and fruit mixture. Mix thoroughly. Spread batter in well-greased 15 x 10 x 1-inch (37 x 25 x 2.5 cm) jelly roll pan. Bake 30 minutes. Brush with orange glaze while warm, if desired. Cool; cut into bars.

Orange Glaze

1/2 cup (125 ml) sugar

1/4 cup (50 ml) orange juice

Combine sugar and orange juice in small saucepan. Heat, stirring constantly, just until sugar dissolves.
Yield: 3-4 dozen

ZUCCHINI CAKE

This tasty squash has now become very popular as an ingredient in this wonderfully spicy cake. Complemented by a tangy Orange Icing it becomes a worthy gift as well as a fine ending to a hearty meal.

2 medium zucchini
2-1/2 cups (625 ml) all-purpose flour
2 teaspoons (10 ml) baking powder
1 teaspoon (5 ml) baking soda
1 teaspoon (5 ml) salt
2 teaspoons (10 ml) cinnamon
1/2 teaspoon (2 ml) ground cloves

3 eggs
1/2 cup (125 ml) vegetable oil
1-1/3 cups (325 ml) sugar
1/2 cup (125 ml) orange juice
1 teaspoon (5 ml) almond extract
Orange Icing

Preheat oven to 350° F. (180° C.). Assemble Salad Maker with Shredding Disc. Shred zucchini, enough to make about 1-1/2 cups (375 ml). Set aside. In large bowl mix flour, baking powder, baking soda, salt, cinnamon and cloves. Set aside. Assemble Mixer. In large mixer bowl beat eggs at #4. Stir in oil, sugar, orange juice, almond extract and shredded zucchini. Mix well, adjusting speed as necessary. Add flour mixture, stirring just to moisten. Pour into greased 13 x 9 x 2-inch (33 x 23 x 5 cm) pan. Bake for 35-40 minutes, or until cake tests done. Cool in pan on rack.

Orange Icing

2 tablespoons (30 ml) butter or
    margarine, softened
3 cups (750 ml) confectioners' sugar

1/4 cup (50 ml) orange juice
2 teaspoons (10 ml) lemon juice

Assemble Mixer. In small mixer bowl beat all the ingredients together at #4 until well blended. If consistency of icing is a little thick, thin with a little more orange juice.
Yield: 12-15 servings

MOCHA BALLS

Nuts, maraschino cherries and the intermingled flavors of coffee and chocolate make this an irresistible cookie.

1 cup (250 ml) nuts
1/2 cup (125) maraschino cherries
1 cup (250 ml) butter, softened
1/2 cup (125 ml) sugar
2 teaspoons (10 ml) vanilla extract

1-3/4 cups (450 ml) all-purpose flour
1/4 cup (50 ml) cocoa
1 tablespoon (15 ml) instant coffee
1/4 teaspoon (1 ml) salt
Confectioners' sugar

Preheat oven to 325° F. (160° C.). Assemble Blender. Blender-chop nuts and drained maraschino cherries. Set aside. Assemble Mixer. Cream butter in large mixer bowl at #4. Gradually add sugar and vanilla extract. Continue beating until well blended. Sift together flour, cocoa, coffee and salt. Gradually add to creamed mixture, adjusting speed as needed (probably #6). Blend in nuts and cherries. Chill dough for ease in handling. Shape into 1-inch (2.5 cm) balls. Place on ungreased cookie sheets. Bake 20 minutes. Remove to wire rack. While still warm, dust cookies with confectioners' sugar.
Yield: About 6 dozen

STANDARD PASTRY

1 cup (250 ml) all-purpose flour
1/2 teaspoon (2 ml) salt

1/3 cup (75 ml) shortening
2-3 tablespoons (30-45 ml) cold water

Assemble Mixer. Put all ingredients except water into large mixer bowl. Mix on speed #1 until mixture resembles coarse meal. Add water, 1 tablespoon (15 ml) at a time, and mix as little as possible. Form into ball. Roll out onto a floured pastry cloth. Bake at 475° F. (250° C.) for 8-10 minutes.
Yield: 1 8-inch (20 cm) pie crust

BUTTERY NUT CRUST

1/2 cup (125 ml) nuts, chopped
1 cup (250 ml) all-purpose flour
4 tablespoons (60 ml) brown sugar

1/2 teaspoon (2 ml) cinnamon
1/2 cup (125 ml) butter, melted

Heat oven to 325° F. (160° C.). Assemble Mixer. Put nuts, flour, brown sugar and cinnamon into small mixer bowl. With mixer at #1 gradually add butter. Mix until dry ingredients are moistened and crumbly. Pat into a 9-inch (23 cm) pie pan. Bake 25 minutes. Cool before filling.

Yield: 1 9-inch (23 cm) pie shell

NOTE: For crumb crust pies, prepare crumb bases of bread, crackers, cookies or nuts, using Blender or Shredding Disc of Salad Maker.

DELUXE PECAN PIE

Sweet and rich, pecan pie is a Southern favorite from the earliest days of pecan growing. It is now part of the American culinary heritage.

3 eggs
1 cup (250 ml) dark or light corn syrup
1 cup (250 ml) sugar
2 tablespoons (30 ml) butter or
    margarine, melted

1 teaspoon (5 ml) vanilla extract
Dash salt
1 cup (250 ml) pecans
1 9-inch (23 cm) unbaked pie shell

Assemble Mixer. In large mixer bowl beat eggs slightly; mix in corn syrup, sugar, butter, vanilla extract and salt. Blend well. Add pecans. Pour into unbaked pie shell. Bake at 400° F. (200° C.) for 15 minutes. Reduce oven temperature to 350° F. (180° C.). Bake for 30-35 minutes longer.

Yield: 6-8 servings

CHOCOLATE CHEESE PIE

Just before serving, dribble a little chocolate sauce over each wedge and top with grated chocolate.

1 cup (250 ml) sugar
3 packages (8 ounces or 227 g each)
    cream cheese, softened
5 eggs

1 tablespoon (15 ml) vanilla extract
1 package (4 ounces or 113 g) sweet
    chocolate, melted and cooled
1 tablespoon (15 ml) lemon juice

Assemble Mixer. In large mixer bowl, add sugar to cheese and beat at #4. Beat in eggs, one at a time, and add vanilla extract. Measure 2 cups (500 ml) of the cheese mixture; fold melted chocolate into it. Add lemon juice to remaining cheese mixture, and pour into buttered 10-inch (25 cm) pie pan. Top with chocolate mixture. Bake at 350° F. (180° C.) for 40-45 minutes. Cool; then chill. Cut in wedges.
Yield: 8 servings

RAISIN PIE

This has to be the prettiest raisin cake ever! The texture is very rich with the meringue adding a glamorous touch. For best results, all meringue pies should be cooled on wire racks away from drafts.

4 eggs
2 cups (500 ml) sour cream
2 cups (500 ml) sugar
4 teaspoons (20 ml) all-purpose flour

1-1/2 cups (375 ml) raisins
1 9-inch (23 cm) baked pie shell
8 tablespoons (120 ml) sugar

Preheat oven to 400° F. (200° C.). Separate eggs. Put the yolks in a saucepan; add sour cream, sugar, flour and raisins. Mix thoroughly, and cook until thick. Pour mixture into baked pastry shell. Assemble Mixer. In small mixer bowl beat egg whites with 8 tablespoons (120 ml) sugar at #9 to form meringue. Spoon onto pie, sealing meringue to crust. Bake 5-7 minutes until browned.
Yield: 1 9-inch (23 cm) pie

MANDARIN ORANGE PIE

This recipe comes to us from a friend who tasted it in Tokyo and just had to have it in her own home. It's a delicious and unusual Oriental adaptation.

1 envelope unflavored gelatin
2 tablespoons (30 ml) cold water
1 cup (250 ml) boiling water
1 cup (250 ml) sugar
1/2 cup (125 ml) lemon juice

1 cup (250 ml) heavy cream
1 can (11 ounces or 309 g) mandarin
   oranges, drained
1 9-inch (23 cm) baked pastry shell
Orange slices

Soften gelatin in cold water. Stir in boiling water. Add sugar and stir until dissolved. Add lemon juice and stir. Refrigerate until slightly thickened but not set. Assemble Mixer. In small mixer bowl whip cream until thick at #10. Fold into gelatin mixture. Add mandarin oranges and stir gently until evenly distributed. Pour into baked pastry shell. Garnish with orange slices. Chill 4 hours.
Yield: 1 9-inch (23 cm) pie

SOUR CREAM APPLE PIE

4 cups (1000 ml) peeled, cored and
   chopped apples
1 cup (250 ml) sour cream
1 cup (250 ml) sugar
3 tablespoons (45 ml) all-purpose flour
1/4 teaspoon (1 ml) salt
1 teaspoon (5 ml) vanilla extract

1 egg
1 9-inch (23 cm) pastry shell, unbaked
1/3 cup (75 ml) firmly packed dark
   brown sugar
1/2 cup (125 ml) all-purpose flour
1/4 cup (50 ml) butter

Assemble Blender. Blender-chop apples. Set aside. Assemble Mixer. Beat together at #4 the sour cream, sugar, flour, salt, vanilla extract, egg. Pour into unbaked pastry shell. Add apples. Bake at 375° F. (190° C.) for 25 minutes. Mix brown sugar, flour and butter. Sprinkle on top of pie. Bake 10-15 minutes more.
Yield: 1 9-inch (23 cm) pie

STRAWBERRY CHIFFON PIE

Voted one of the best chiffons by the authors because it has such good "body" and a delicious strawberry flavor. This pie is a winner.

1 box (3 ounces or 84 g) strawberry
    gelatin
2/3 cup (175 ml) boiling water
Dash salt
2 tablespoons (30 ml) lemon juice

1 package (10 ounces or 280 g) frozen
    sliced strawberries, thawed
3 egg whites
1/3 cup (75 ml) sugar
Ladyfinger Crust

Dissolve gelatin in boiling water. Add salt, lemon juice and strawberries. Chill until thickened but not firm. Assemble Mixer. In small mixer bowl beat egg whites at #9 until foamy; gradually add sugar and beat until stiff but not dry. Fold into gelatin. Pile into ladyfinger crust, and chill until firm.

Ladyfinger Crust

12 ladyfingers

2 tablespoons (30 ml) butter, melted

Split the ladyfingers. Use some to line the bottom of a 9-inch (23 cm) pie pan. Cut some into halves crosswise and arrange around edge of pan. Break remainder into small pieces and fill in spaces in bottom of pan. Pour melted butter over ladyfingers on bottom. Chill.
Yield: 6-8 servings

Chapter Nine
JAMS, JELLIES, PRESERVES

STRAWBERRY BUTTER

This long loved spread is delicious on toast, pancakes and waffles.

3-1/4 cups (825 ml) fresh strawberries
2 tablespoons (30 ml) lemon juice

1/2 cup (125 ml) honey
1/2 to 3/4 cups (125-200 ml) butter

Assemble Blender. Put strawberries and lemon juice into blender container and process at PUREE. Pour into saucepan with honey, and slowly bring to a boil. Reduce heat and simmer 20-30 minutes, stirring occasionally. Add butter to the hot sauce. Pour into a pitcher and serve.
Yield: 1-3/4 cups (450 ml)

CHOP SUEY PICKLES

Red and green peppers add a special touch in this recipe.

6 large cucumbers, peeled and
   thin-sliced
10 medium onions, thin-sliced
3 large green peppers
3 large sweet red peppers
1/2 cup (125 ml) salt
Cold water

2 cups (500 ml) vinegar
3 tablespoons (45 ml) pickling spices
1 cup (250 ml) water
4 cups (1000 ml) sugar
2 tablespoons (30 ml) celery salt
1 teaspoon (5 ml) curry powder

Assemble Salad Maker. Slice cucumbers, onions as indicated above. Assemble Blender. Water-chop peppers. Combine with cucumbers and onions. Sprinkle with salt and add enough cold water to cover vegetables. Let stand overnight. Drain thoroughly. Add the vinegar, pickling spices, water, sugar and celery salt. Boil 10 minutes. Add curry powder at the last minute. Pack into hot, sterilized pint jars, leaving 1/2-inch (1 cm) headroom. Process in boiling water bath 5 minutes.
Yield: 8 pints (4 liters)

PEANUT BUTTER

Children's favorite gourmet spread was never better than when it's created homemade in moments.

1-1/2 cups (375 ml) salted peanuts

Assemble Blender. Put peanuts into blender container, cover and process at BLEND to the desired consistency. If necessary, STOP BLENDER, use rubber spatula to keep mixture around the processing blades.
Yield: 3/4 cup (200 ml)

GARDEN MUSTARD PICKLES

6 pickling cucumbers
2 large green peppers, halved
    and seeded
2 large red peppers, halved, seeded
1 small cauliflower, separated into
    flowerets
1 pound (0.5 kg) small white onions,
    peeled
6 green tomatoes, cut into wedges
1/3 cup (75 ml) kosher salt

1/2 cup (50 ml) firmly packed light
    brown sugar
3 tablespoons (45 ml) dry mustard
1-1/2 teaspoons (7 ml) turmeric
2 teaspoons (10 ml) mustard seeds
2 teaspoons (10 ml) celery seeds
6 cups (1.5 liters) cider vinegar
1/2 cup (125 ml) all-purpose flour
1 cup (250 ml) cold water

Assemble Salad Maker. Thick-slice cucumbers and peppers. Combine with cauliflower, onions and tomato in large glass bowl. Sprinkle with kosher salt. Stir to blend well. Cover bowl with plastic wrap and let stand about 12 hours at room temperature. Then pour off all liquid and put into large kettle. Add brown sugar, mustard, turmeric, mustard seeds and celery seeds. Stir in cider vinegar.

Bring to a boil, stirring often. Then lower heat and simmer 15 minutes. Combine flour and cold water in small bowl and mix to paste. Stir slowly into bubbling liquid. Cook, stirring constantly, until mixture thickens and bubbles about 3 minutes. Ladle into hot, sterilized pint (500 ml) jars, leaving 1/2-inch (1 cm) headroom. Seal and process in boiling water bath 10 minutes.
Yield: 8 pints (4 liters)

SWEET CUCUMBER RELISH

6 cucumbers, seeded
3 medium onions, peeled
3 tablespoons (45 ml) kosher salt
1/4 cup (50 ml) finely chopped
    preserved ginger
1 cup (250 ml) cider vinegar

1/2 cup (125 ml) firmly packed light
    brown sugar
1/2 teaspoon (2 ml) cinnamon
1/2 teaspoon (2 ml) dry mustard
Salt, optional

Assemble Food Grinder with Coarse Disc. Grind cucumbers and onions. Mix with salt in glass or porcelain bowl. Let stand, uncovered, about 12 hours. Drain well and place in saucepan with remaining ingredients. Taste for saltiness. Add salt, if desired. Bring quickly to a boil and boil rapidly 10 minutes, stirring occasionally. Spoon at once into hot, sterilized jars. Seal. Store at least 4 weeks.
Yield: 5 half pints (1.25 liters)

SPICED PEAR BUTTER

A combination of spices give this spread its rich flavor. It's very good on hot bread or biscuits.

12 fresh pears
1/4 cup (50 ml) cider vinegar
1/4 cup (50 ml) water
4 cups (1000 ml) sugar

1/2 cup (125 ml) orange juice
1/4 cup (50 ml) lemon juice
1-1/2 teaspoons (7 ml) whole allspice
    tied in a cheesecloth

Pare and core pears; cut into 1-inch (2.5 cm) cubes, enough to make 3 quarts (3 liters). Place in large kettle with cider vinegar and water. Cook, covered, until soft, about 30 minutes. Assemble Blender. Pour soft pears into blender container. Cover and process at PUREE. Measure pulp. There should be about 7 cups (1,750 ml). Return to kettle. Add sugar, orange juice, lemon juice and allspice. Cook over medium heat, stirring frequently until mixture is very thick, about 2 hours. Remove allspice. Ladle into hot, sterilized jars, leaving 1/2-inch (1 cm) headspace. Seal.
Yield: 6 half pints (1.5 liters)

BERRY FRUIT RELISH

4 cups (1 liter) cranberries
2 small oranges, quartered

1-1/2 cups (375 ml) sugar
1-1/2 cups (375 ml) chopped pitted dates

Assemble Food Grinder with Coarse Disc. Grind cranberries and oranges. Stir in sugar and pitted dates. Cover, and chill until ready to serve.
Yield: 1 quart (1 liter)

ZUCCHINI PICKLES

Looking for an unusual sandwich pickle? Just try zucchini. Let the food processor do all the slicing.

5 pounds (2.5 kg) zucchini, unpeeled
   and thin-sliced
4-5 medium onions, thin-sliced
1 quart (1 liter) vinegar
2 cups (500 ml) sugar

1/4 cup (50 ml) salt
2 teaspoons (10 ml) celery seed
2 teaspoons (10 ml) turmeric
1 teaspoon (5 ml) dry mustard

Assemble Salad Maker. Slice zucchini at speed #8 and onions at speed #6 as indicated above. Combine rest of ingredients in saucepan. Bring to a boil. Pour over zucchini and onions. Let stand 1 hour, stirring occasionally. In kettle, bring mixture to a boil; then simmer 3 minutes. Continue simmering while pouring into hot, sterilized pint jars, one at a time. Leave 1/2-inch (1 cm) headroom, making sure that vinegar solution covers vegetables. Seal and process in boiling water bath 15 minutes.
Yield: Approximately 8 pints (4 liters)

RED PEPPER RELISH

12 large sweet red peppers, cut
    into quarters
1 tablespoon (15 ml) salt

2 cups (500 ml) vinegar
3 cups (750 ml) sugar

Assemble Food Grinder with Coarse Disc. Grind red peppers. Put into glass bowl and sprinkle with salt. Cover loosely with plastic wrap, and let stand about 12 hours. Drain well. Combine in kettle with vinegar and sugar. Bring to a boil and cook rapidly, uncovered, stirring often about 45 minutes, or until thick. Pour out at once into hot, sterilized jars, leaving 1/4-inch (0.6 cm) headroom. Seal. Process in boiling water bath 10 minutes.
Yield: 5-6 half pints (1.25-1.5 liters)

FESTIVE CRANBERRY RELISH

The cranberry is a native American fruit which the Indians were eating long before the Pilgrims arrived in 1620. Today it is a symbol of the Thanksgiving holiday and a superb accompaniment to chicken and turkey dishes. Much easier to prepare now that you have help with the grinding and chopping.

1/2 cup (125 ml) walnuts
4 cups (1 liter) fresh cranberries
2 medium oranges, unpeeled

1-1/2 cups (375 ml) firmly-packed light
    brown sugar

Assemble Blender. Blender-chop walnuts and set aside. Wash and pick over cranberries. Cut oranges into wedges, taking out seeds. Assemble Food Grinder with Coarse Disc. Grind cranberries and oranges. Stir in light brown sugar and walnuts. Chill before serving.
Yield: 1 quart (1 liter)

LEMON-PEAR HONEY

Delicious on toasted English muffins.

6 large ripe pears, pared and cored   5 cups (1250 ml) sugar
1 lemon, thinly sliced

Place large pan under food grinder head. Using Coarse Disc, grind pears. Add lemon and sugar. Cook and stir until boiling. Reduce heat, cover and simmer until thickened and clear, about 40-50 minutes. Ladle into hot canning jars, leaving 1/2-inch head space. Seal. Process in simmering water bath 10 minutes.
Yield: 6 1/2-pint jars (1.5 liters)

CARROT ALMOND PRESERVE

A "conserve" always has either nuts or raisins in it. They are not as common as jams and preserves but just as good.

2 pounds (1 kg) carrots   1/2 teaspoon (2 ml) salt
4 cups (1 liter) water   1-1/3 cups (325 ml) slivered blanched
2 lemons   almonds
4 cups (1000 ml) sugar

Assemble Food Grinder with Coarse Disc. Grind carrots. Put in kettle with water, and cook, covered, for 10 minutes or until almost tender. Do not drain. Grind lemons, and add to carrots. Add sugar and salt. Cook rapidly for 25 minutes, or until thick, stirring occasionally. Add almonds and pour into hot, sterilized pint jars. Seal at once.
Yield: 4 pints (2 liters)

ROSE PETAL JAM

3/4 cup (200 ml) water
1 cup (250 ml) rose petals, firmly packed
    (snip white inside portion of petal)
2 tablespoons (30 ml) lemon juice

2-1/2 cups (625 ml) sugar
3/4 cup (200 ml) water
1 1-3/4-ounce (49 g) package powdered
    fruit pectin

Assemble Blender. Put water, rose petals and lemon juice in blender container. Cover and process at LIQUEFY until smooth. Gradually add the sugar; blend until dissolved. Into a large pan put remaining water and pectin; bring to a boil. Boil 1 minute. Add rose mixture and continue to boil for 3 minutes. Remove from heat. Skim and stir for 5 minutes. Ladle in sterilized jars; seal. Store in refrigerator for up to a month or store in freezer.
Yield: 2 pints (1 liter)

STRAWBERRY-RHUBARB JAM

2 thick stalks rhubarb, about
    18 inches (45 cm) long
1 quart (1 liter) strawberries, hulled
    and washed
2 tablespoons (30 ml) lemon juice

1/4 teaspoon (1 ml) salt
1 1-3/4-ounce (49 g) package powdered
    fruit pectin
5-1/2 cups (1300 ml) sugar
12 drops red food coloring

Place large pan under food grinder head. Using Coarse Disc, grind rhubarb and strawberries. Add lemon juice, salt and pectin. Cook and stir until boiling. Add sugar and food coloring. Stirring constantly, boil 1 minute. Turn off heat source. Stir and skim 5 minutes. Ladle into hot canning jars, leaving 1/2-inch (1.2 cm) head-space. Seal and process in simmering water bath 10 minutes.
Yield: 6 pints (3 liters)

Chapter Ten
MISCELLANEOUS

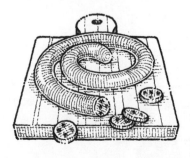

EGGNOG

8 eggs
2 quarts (2 liters) milk
8 teaspoons (40 ml) sugar

4 teaspoons (20 ml) vanilla extract
Dash salt
Nutmeg

Assemble Mixer. In large mixer bowl beat eggs at #4. Add remaining ingredients, and mix well. Pour into serving glasses or mugs; sprinkle with nutmeg.
Yield: 16 4-ounce (100 ml) servings

DAIQUIRI

1/3 cup (75 ml) frozen limeade
  concentrate, thawed
4 jiggers light Bacardi rum

1-1/2 cups (375 ml) crushed ice or 6 whole
  ice cubes

Assemble Blender. Put all ingredients into blender container, cover and process at LIQUEFY a few seconds. Strain into cocktail glasses.

VARIATION:

FROZEN DAIQUIRI
Double the amount of ice and continue to blend until sherbet consistency.
Mound into glasses and serve with straws.
Yield: 4 3-ounce (75 ml) drinks

CRANBERRY FRUIT DRINK

3 cups (750 ml) cranberry juice,
   chilled
1 small banana, sliced
1/4 cup (50 ml) crushed pineapple
1/4 cup (50 ml) diced melon (cantaloupe
   or honeydew)

4 strawberries, hulled
6 sections mandarin orange
8 ice cubes, coarsley cracked

Assemble Blender. Place all ingredients in blender container; cover and process at FRAPPE until very smooth. Pour into glasses, and serve at once.
Yield: 4 6-ounce (150 ml) servings

ORANGE SMOOTHIE

1 large orange, peeled and cut
   into chunks
1/2 cup (125 ml) orange juice

1 pint (500 ml) vanilla ice cream
Thin orange slices

Assemble Blender. Place all ingredients except thin orange slices in blender container. Cover and process at WHIP until smooth. Pour into 4 stemmed glasses. Garnish with thin orange slices.
Yield: 4 6-ounce (150 ml) servings

MAUI MIST

1 cup (250 ml) pineapple juice
1 banana, broken into 4 pieces
1 teaspoon (5 ml) lemon juice

2 teaspoons (10 ml) sugar
Dash of salt
1-1/2 cups (375 ml) crushed ice

Assemble Blender. Put all ingredients into blender container, cover and process at LIQUEFY until slushy.
Yield: 3 cups (0.75 liter)

GRASSHOPPER

2 jiggers white Creme de Cacao
1 jigger green Creme de Menthe
1 jigger heavy cream

3/4 cup (200 ml) crushed ice or 3 whole
    ice cubes

Assemble Blender. Put all ingredients into blender container. Cover and process at LIQUEFY a few seconds. Strain into cocktail glasses.
Yield: 2 4-ounce (100 ml) drinks

VARIATIONS:

Use 3 cups (0.75 liter) ice cream in place of cream and ice. Blend until smooth for after-dinner dessert drink.
PINK SQUIRREL: Use 1 jigger Creme de Noyaux instead of Creme de Menthe and use cream and ice or ice cream.

BRANDY ALEXANDER FRAPPES

2 tablespoons (30 ml) brandy
2 tablespoons (30 ml) Creme de Cacao

3 cups (0.75 liter) softened vanilla
ice cream

Assemble Blender. Put brandy and Creme de Cacao into blender. Add ice cream, spooning it into the container by tablespoonfuls. Cover and process at LIQUEFY until smooth and sherbet-like consistency. Pour into chilled sherbet glasses and top with chocolate curls.
Yield: 2 3-ounce (84 g) drinks

ITALIAN STALLION

2 jiggers Galliano
1 cup (250 ml) orange juice
2 eggs

2 ice cubes
1 ripe banana, cut in 6 pieces

Assemble Blender. Put all ingredients into container in order listed. Cover and process at LIQUEFY until smooth.
Yield: 4 6-ounce (150 ml) servings

ORANGE FLUFFY FROSTING

1/3 cup (75 ml) butter, softened
1 teaspoon (5 ml) vanilla extract
1/4 teaspoon (1 ml) salt
2 tablespoons (30 ml) grated orange rind

2 egg whites
1 pound (454 g) confectioners' sugar
1 tablespoon (15 ml) milk

Assemble Mixer. Cream butter, vanilla extract, salt and grated orange rind at #4 until light. Add egg whites and confectioners' sugar, a little at a time, beating well after each addition. Add milk and beat. If necessary, add more milk to make desired consistency.
Yield: 2 cups (500 ml)

BUTTER CREAM FROSTING

1 pound (454 g) confectioners' sugar
Dash salt
1 teaspoon (5 ml) vanilla extract

1/4 cup (50 ml) milk
1/3 cup (75 ml) butter, softened

Assemble Mixer. Put sugar, salt, vanilla extract and milk into large mixer bowl and blend at #4 until smooth. Add butter and beat at #8 until smooth. Add more milk if thinner consistency is desired. If chocolate butter cream is desired, add 2 squares (2 ounces or 56 g) unsweetened baking chocolate, melted and cooled.
Yield: 2 cups (500 ml)

BANANA SAUCE

2 ripe bananas, peeled
Juice of 1/2 lemon

2 tablespoons (30 ml) sugar
1/2 cup (125 ml) heavy cream

Assemble Blender. Place all ingredients in blender container. Cover and process at BLEND until completely smooth. Serve over fruit salads.
Yield: 1-1/4 cups (300 ml)

HOLLANDAISE

1/2 cup (125 ml) butter or margarine
4 egg yolks
2-3 tablespoons (30-45 ml) fresh
    lemon juice

1/4 teaspoon (1 ml) salt
Dash pepper

Heat butter or margarine until bubbly. Assemble Blender. Place egg yolks, fresh lemon juice, salt and pepper in blender container. Cover and process quickly at MIX. Remove feeder cap and pour bubbly butter in a thin but steady stream. Serve immediately. This sauce is particularly good over broccoli, asparagus, grilled tomatoes or fish.
Yield: 1 cup (250 ml)

BARBECUE SAUCE

1/2 cup (125 ml) tomato catsup
1/2 teaspoon (2 ml) fresh grated
    lemon peel
2 teaspoons (10 ml) lemon juice

2 teaspoons (10 ml) Worcestershire sauce
1-1/2 teaspoons (7 ml) prepared mustard
Dash onion powder

Assemble Blender. Place all ingredients in blender container; cover and process at MIX until well blended. Use to baste hamburgers, spareribs, hot dogs and chicken. Yield: 2/3 cup (175 ml)

BASIC WHITE SAUCE

1 tablespoon (15 ml) butter and 1 tablespoon (15 ml) all-purpose flour for each cup of milk or cream. (For thicker sauce, use 2 tablespoons [30 ml] butter and 2 tablespoons [30 ml] all-purpose flour per cup of milk or cream. Increase the proportions to 3-4 tablespoons [45-60 ml] butter and 3-4 tablespoons [45-60 ml] all-purpose flour for each cup of milk or cream for a very thick sauce.)

Assemble Blender. Put ingredients into blender container, cover and process at WHIP until well blended. Pour into saucepan and cook over low heat, stirring constantly until thick. Season to taste with salt and pepper.

HARD SAUCE

1/2 cup (125 ml) butter, softened   1 teaspoon (5 ml) vanilla extract
1-1/2 cups (375 ml) confectioners' sugar

    Assemble Mixer. Cream butter with confectioners' sugar at #4 until light and fluffy. Add vanilla extract. Chill. Serve with puddings. A little brandy or rum flavoring may be added to give it a little more zest.
Yield: 1-1/2 cups (375 ml)

ORANGE BUTTER SAUCE

4 egg yolks   2 tablespoons (30 ml) brandy
2 tablespoons (30 ml) orange   1/4 pound (125 ml) melted butter
    marmalade

    Assemble Blender. Put all ingredients except butter into blender container, cover and process at MIX until blended. Remove feeder cap and add melted butter in slow steady stream until mixture is creamy and slightly thick. Spread on cooked crepe and roll. Pour heated cognac over crepes, and flame!
Yield: 1 cup (250 ml)

ALMOND NOUGAT

2 cups (500 ml) sugar
1 cup (250 ml) light corn syrup
1/2 cup (125 ml) water
2 egg whites

3 tablespoons (45 ml) butter or margarine,
    softened
3 tablespoons (10 ml) vanilla extract
1 cup (250 ml) golden raisins
1 cup (250 ml) roasted almonds*

Assemble Blender. Blender-chop 1/2 cup whole blanched almonds in the Mini-Blend jar. Repeat until 1 cup chopped nuts is obtained. Combine sugar, corn syrup and water in saucepan; cook over low heat, stirring until sugar is dissolved. Cover and cook 5 minutes to dissolve any sugar crystals on sides of pan. Uncover and cook over medium heat without stirring to hard ball stage (about 260° F. or 110° C.).

Assemble Mixer. In a large mixer bowl, beat egg whites at #9 until they are stiff. Gradually pour about half of the hot syrup over them beating continuously about 5 minutes, until the mass thickens, then return remaining syrup to heat and boil to hard-crack stage (about 300° F. or 150° C.). Pour over first mixture, beating again. Continue beating until thick. Stir in butter, vanilla extract, raisins and roasted almonds. Turn into lightly buttered 8-inch (20 cm) square pan. Allow to set thoroughly. Cut into squares, and wrap individually in waxed paper.

Yield: 40 pieces

*To roast almonds, spread 1/2 teaspoon butter, margarine, peanut or vegetable oil over surface of shallow pan. Add almonds in single layer. Roast, stirring often, at 300° F. (150° C.) for 15 minutes or until they turn color. Do not wait for them to become golden brown. The heat in the nuts will continue to roast them after they are out of the oven.

ALMOND FIG CANDY

8 ounces (227 g) almond paste
8 ounces (227 g) dried figs

1 tablespoon (15 ml) brandy extract
Confectioners' sugar

Assemble Grinder with Fine Disc. Put dried figs through food grinder. Add almond paste and brandy extract. Blend well. Shape into 3/4-inch (1.8 cm) balls. Use small amounts of sugar on hands if mixture is sticky. Roll balls in confectioners' sugar. Store airtight in single layers between sheets of waxed paper in cool dry place. Yield: 40 pieces

FRUIT-PASTE CANDY

Peel of 1 medium orange
1 cup (250 ml) pecans
1 cup (250 ml) dried apricots
1 cup (250 ml) raisins
1 cup (250 ml) pitted dates

1/2 cup (125 ml) flaked coconut
2 tablespoons (30 ml) honey,
   approximately
1/4 teaspoon (1 ml) salt
Tinted coconut

Assemble Blender. Blender-grate orange peel. Assemble Grinder with Coarse Disc. Combine pecans, apricots, raisins, dates and coconut; put through food grinder. Stir in enough honey to make mixture stick together. Mix in grated orange peel and salt. Mix well. With wet hands, form into balls using a rounded teaspoon (5-10 ml) for each ball. Flatten slightly. Roll in tinted coconut. Wrap each piece in plastic wrap, and store in an airtight container.

Tinted Coconut

1 cup (250 ml) flaked coconut
Few drops food coloring

1/4 teaspoon (1 ml) cold water

To tint coconut, sprinkle flaked coconut on waxed paper. Mix a few drops food coloring with cold water. Sprinkle on coconut, and mix until tinted. Let dry. Yield: 60 pieces

NO-BAKE NUT CONFECTION

2/3 cup (175 ml) maraschino cherries
1-1/2 cups (375 ml) walnuts
32 vanilla wafers
1/3 cup (75 ml) sugar
Dash salt

1/2 teaspoon (2 ml) cinnamon
1 teaspoon (5 ml) lemon juice
2/3 cup (175 ml) sweetened
    condensed milk
Confectioners' sugar

    Assemble Blender. Blender-chop maraschino cherries and walnuts. Set aside. Assemble Salad Maker with Shredding Disc. Crumb vanilla wafers at #6. Assemble Mixer. In large mixer bowl blend together at #4 the vanilla wafer crumbs, sugar, salt, cinnamon, maraschino cherries and walnuts. Add lemon juice and condensed milk. Blend well. Form into balls, and roll in confectioners' sugar.
Yield: 2 dozen

SPICY NUTS

1-1/2 cups (375 ml) confectioners' sugar
2 tablespoons (30 ml) cornstarch
1 teaspoon (5 ml) cinnamon
1/2 teaspoon (2 ml) cloves
1/4 teaspoon (1 ml) allspice

Dash salt
2 tablespoons (30 ml) grated orange peel
2 egg whites
3 tablespoons (45 ml) orange juice
2 cups (500 ml) walnut or pecan halves

    Sift together confectioners' sugar, cornstarch, cinnamon, cloves, allspice and salt; stir in grated orange peel. Assemble Mixer. In small mixer bowl beat egg whites at #4 until foamy. Blend with orange juice. Stir in nuts, coating well. Drain thoroughly; then roll in sugar mixture to coat well. Spread on cookie sheet, not allowing nuts to touch one another. Bake at 250° F. (110° C.) for 20-25 minutes, or until dry. Cool before storing in covered container.
Yield: 3 cups (750 ml)

CREPES

1-1/2 cups (375 ml) milk
2 tablespoons (30 ml) vegetable oil
3 eggs

1-1/2 cups (375 ml) all-purpose flour
Dash salt

Assemble Blender. Pour all ingredients into blender container in order listed. Cover and process at BLEND until smooth. Brush a 7-inch crepe skillet with oil and place over moderate heat. Pour 2-3 tablespoons of batter into skillet and tilt the pan in all directions so that batter thinly covers bottom of skillet. Cook until bottom is lightly browned and top of crepe is dry. Turn crepe carefully and cook a few seconds longer. Remove from skillet and stack on a platter, putting paper towels between them to keep them from sticking. Crepes can be wrapped in plastic wrap and stored in the refrigerator, or if they are being made a month or two in advance, wrap in freezer wrap and store in freezer.

Yield: 20-24 crepes

VARIATIONS:

Parmesan Crepes:

Add 1/2 cup (125 ml) grated Parmesan cheese to basic crepe recipe. Stir frequently while preparing crepes.

Whole Wheat Crepes:

Use 1-1/4 cups (300 ml) whole wheat flour instead of all-purpose flour. Add 2 tablespoons (30 ml) wheat germ to the basic crepe recipe.

Herb Crepes:

Add 1 teaspoon (5 ml) oregano or thyme or 3 sprigs fresh parsley to basic crepe recipe.

Corn Meal Crepes:

Add 1/2 cup (125 ml) corn meal to basic crepe recipe. Stir frequently.

CREPES SUZETTES

1/2 cup (125 ml) soft butter
1/2 cup (125 ml) sugar
2 teaspoons (10 ml) grated orange rind
1/3 cup (75 ml) orange juice
1 teaspoon (5 ml) lemon juice

2 tablespoons (30 ml) sugar
2 tablespoons (30 ml) brandy
1/2 cup (125 ml) brandy
Crepes (see page 139)

Blend first 5 ingredients. Spread on crepes and roll or fold. Put in chafing dish or skillet over low heat. Sprinkle with 2 tablespoons (30 ml) sugar and 2 tablespoons (30 ml) brandy. Warm 1/2 cup (125 ml) brandy. Pour over crepes and ignite with a long tapered match.

Yield: sauce for 16 crepes

KIELBASA SAUSAGE

3 pounds boneless pork butt or
    pork shoulder, cut into 1-inch
    (2.5 cm) cubes
1 pound veal, cut into 1-inch
    (2.5 cm) cubes
1 tablespoon (15 ml) marjoram

3 garlic cloves, crushed with a
    garlic press
3 teaspoons (15 ml) salt
1 teaspoon (5 ml) pepper
1/4 teaspoon (1 ml) ground allspice

Sprinkle combined seasonings over meat cubes in a large bowl. Toss until well coated. Grind with coarse grinding disc, and stuff into casings using medium stuffing tube according to Oster Sausage Stuffing Kit instructions.
Yield: About 32 4-inch (10 cm) sausages

ROSE'S SPECIAL COUNTRY SAUSAGE

With the Oster Sausage Stuffing Kit, you can make delicious homemade sausages in a matter of minutes. See specific instructions for sausage making. This recipe yields an unusual savory sausage which can be made into breakfast links with the small stuffing tube or into large sausage with the medium stuffing tube.

2-1/2 pounds (1.3 kg) lean country
    ribs or pork loin end roast, cut
    into 1-inch (2.5 cm) cubes
2 teaspoons (10 ml) salt
1 teaspoon (5 ml) pepper

1/2 teaspoon (2 ml) ground ginger
1/2 teaspoon (2 ml) poultry seasoning
1/2 teaspoon (2 ml) sugar
1/4 teaspoon (1 ml) ground cloves

Sprinkle combined seasonings over pork cubes in a large bowl. Toss until well coated. Grind and stuff into casings using small stuffing tube according to Oster Sausage Stuffing Kit instructions.
Yield: 30 4-inch (10 cm) breakfast sausages

INDEX

A

almond
  angels, 101
  butter cookies, 106
  fig candy, 137
  nougat, 136
  preserve, carrot, 125
  pretzels, 104
amandine
  broccoli, 59
  celery, 60
antipasto platter, 14
apple
  bread pudding, 89
  cake, quick, 99
  pie, sour cream, 117
  soup, strawberry-blush, 36
apricot custard, 82
asparagus lyonnaise, 62
avocado soup, chilled, 40

B

banana sauce, 133
barbecue sauce, 134
Bavarian cream, strawberry, 83
beef, Indonesian-style, 75
beets, pickled, 64
berry fruit relish, 123
blue cheese dressing, 56
bran pecan squares, 107
brandy Alexander frappes, 131
bread puddings, 87, 89
broccoli amandine, 59
brown sugar cake, 95
brulee, orange creme, 86
butternut bars, 109
butterscotch bread, 24
buttery nut crust, 115

C

cabbage
  salad, 50, 52
  soup, Swedish, 37

canapes, 22
caramel
  custard, 85
  rice pudding, 83
carrot(s)
  almond preserve, 125
  bread, 31
  orange, 65
  oriental, 63
cashew butter, 21
cassoulet, 74
cauliflower
  cream soup, 37
  in cheese puff, 61
  salad, 47
celery
  amandine, 60
  marinated, 50
  seed dressing, 54
cheese
  ball, 12
  cake, creamy, 92
  canapes, 22
  dill bread, 33
  dip base, cottage, 20
  Liptauer, 16
  pie, chocolate, 116
  puff, cauliflower in, 61
  souffle, 13
cherry mold, 49
chestnut mold, 85
chicken
  broiled, 73
  Dijon, 71
  lemon, 69
  liver pate, 15
  mousse, 78
  tarragon, 77

chocolate
    bread pudding, 87
    cheese pie, 116
    chip date cookies, 109
    roll, French, 93
    velvet cake, 98
chop suey pickles, 120
cioppino, 76
clam roll, walnut, 19
coconut chews, 111
coffee cake, raisin, 94
coleslaw, 46
cookies, 101-114
corn
    breads, 25, 27
    pie, 66
cottage cheese dip base, 20
cottage pudding, 84
cranberry
    fruit drink, 129
    festive relish, 124
    molded relish, 51
    salad, whipped, 47
    whole wheat bread, 32
cream (creme)
    Bavarian, 83
    brulee, orange, 86
    minted pots de, 86
    soups, 36, 37, 42
crepes, 139
crescents, sour cream, 27
croquettes, shrimp, 79
cucumber
    relish, sweet, 122
    salad, French country-style, 49
    salad, Hungarian, 45
    yogurt soup, 37
curried fish steaks, 70

D
Daiquiri, 128
dairy dressing, 53
dips, 20
doughnuts, 26, 28
duckling, plum, 68

E
egg spread, smoky, 15
eggnog, 128
eggplant
    casserole, lamb and, 70
    salad spread, 17

F
fish
    curried steaks, 70
    nutty, 71
    patties, fried, 72
French bread, 32
frostings
    butter cream, 132
    orange fluffy, 132
fruit bars, 112
fruit-paste candy, 137

G
ginger
    fruit salad, 44
    pear crumble, 89
gingersnaps, 105
grasshopper, 130
guacamole
    dip, 20
    dressing, 55

H
hard sauce, 135
herb batter bread, 30
herring pate, 13
Hollandaise, 133
honey, lemon-pear, 125

I
Indonesian-style beef, 75
Italian stallion, 131

K
kielbasa sausage, 140

L
lamb
    and eggplant casserole, 70
    cheese pie, 68
Linzer bars, 111
Liptauer cheese, 16
low-cal cottage cheese dip base, 20
lyonnaise, asparagus, 62

M

macaroni pudding, 87
madeleines, 96
mandarin orange pie, 117
maple doughnut holes, 28
marinade, shrimp, 19
marinated
  celery, 50
  mushrooms, 14
Maui mist, 130
mayonnaise, 55
meatballs, Portugese, 75
Mexican tea cookies, 103
mincemeat squares, 102
minestrone, Italian, 38
minted pots de creme, 86
mocha balls, 114
molasses
  corn bread, 27
  sponge cake, 95
mousse
  chicken, 78
  royal pineapple, 88
mushrooms
  marinated, 14
  stuffed, 18
mustard
  sour cream dressing, 54
  pickles, garden, 121

N

no-bake nut confection, 138
nougat, almond, 136
nuts, spicy, 138

O

oatcakes, Canadian, 24
oatmeal bread, 34
onion
  pie, French country, 73
  soup, 39
orange
  butter sauce, 135
  carrots, 65
  cookies, 103
  creme brulee, 86
  fluffy frosting, 132
  perfect salad, 51
  pie, mandarin, 117
  prune nut loaf, 25
  smoothie, 129

P

pastry, standard, 114
pea soup, yellow, 41
peanut butter, 121
pear
  butter, spiced, 122
  crumble, ginger, 89
  honey, lemon, 125
pecan pie, deluxe, 115
pepper relish, red, 124
pickled beets, 64
pickles, 120, 121, 123
piecrust, 114, 115
pineapple
  coffee bread, 31
  mousse, royal, 88
pistachio leaves, 110
plum
  cake, French, 97
  duckling, 68
  whip, 84
poppy seed dressing, 56
pork chops, French country-style, 79
potage Crecy, 38
potato(es)
  cream soup, 42
  French provincial, 60
  puffs, sweet, 58
  salad, hot, 52
  souffle, 62
  spinach soup, 41
pots de creme, minted, 86
potted shrimp, 17
preserve, carrot almond, 125
pretzels, almond, 104
Provencale, tomatoes, 16
prune nut loaf, orange, 25

Q

quiche, salmon zucchini, 77

R

raisin
  coffee cake, 94
  nut drops, 101
  pie, 116

remoulade, shrimp, 80
rolls, French dinner, 33
Roquefort dressing, 56
rose petal jam, 126

S
Sally Lunn, 29
salmon zucchini quiche, 77
sand cake, old-fashioned, 99
sauce aurore, 78
sauerkraut salad, 44
sausages
   country, 140
   hot appetizers, 20
   kielbasa, 140
sea-foam salad, 48
sesame cookies, 107
seviche, 18
shrimp
   croquettes, 79
   marinade, 19
   paste, 12
   potted, 17
   remoulade, 80
slaw, southern, 46
snowcaps, 100
souffles, 13, 62
spinach
   water chestnut canapes, 22
   cream soup, 36
sponge cake, molasses, 95
spread
   eggplant salad, 17
   smoky egg, 15
squares, bran pecan, 107
squash
   bread, 30
   soup, summer, 42
steak tartare, 21
strawberry
   Bavarian cream, 83
   blush apple soup, 36
   butter, 120
   chiffon pie, 118
   rhubarb jam, 126
   tart, French, 82
stuffed mushrooms, 18
summer squash soup, 42

sweet potato puffs, 58
syrup cake, Greek, 97

T
tarragon chicken, 77
tart, French strawberry, 82
tomato(es)
   dressing, 53
   Provencale, 16
   salad, old-fashioned, 48
   soup, Hungarian, 39
trifle, English, 90

V
veal au porto, 69
vegetable
   relish, 65
   soup, 40
   stew, 58
Viennese walnut cookies, 105

W
walnut
   clam roll, 19
   cookies, Viennese, 105
   tea bread, 29
water chestnut canapes, spinach, 22
wheat thins, 108
whip, plum, 84
whipped cranberry salad, 47
whipped cream cake, 95
white sauce, basic, 134
whole wheat bread, cranberry, 32
wilted
   cabbage, 63
   greens, 45

Y
yogurt soup, cucumber, 37

Z
zucchini
   cake, 113
   evergreen, 61
   pickles, 123
   quiche, salmon, 77
   Roman-style, 64
   salad, 46